— FROM —
FARMWORKER
— TO —
ASTRONAUT

MY PATH TO THE STARS

FROM
FARMWORKER
TO
ASTRONAUT

MY PATH TO THE STARS

JOSÉ M. HERNÁNDEZ

PIÑATA BOOKS
ARTE PÚBLICO PRESS
HOUSTON, TEXAS

Piñata Books are full of surprises!

Piñata Books
An imprint of
Arte Público Press
University of Houston
4902 Gulf Fwy, Bldg 19, Rm 100
Houston, Texas 77204-2004

Cover design by Mora Design
(Assistance by Christopher Travis Miller)

Names: Hernández, José M., 1962- author. | Hernández, José M., 1962- From Farmworker to astronaut. | Hernández, José M., 1962- From Farmworker to astronaut. Spanish.
Title: From farmworker to astronaut : my path to the stars = De campesino a astronauta : mi viaje a las estrellas / José M. Hernández. Other titles: De campesino a astronauta
Description: Houston : Arte Público Press, 2019. | Audience: Ages 10-15 | Audience: Grades 7-9 | English and Spanish. | Summary: "Ten-year-old José M. Hernández watched the Apollo 17 moonwalks on his family's black and white television in 1972 and knew what he wanted to be when he grew up: an astronaut. Later that night he told his father and was surprised when his dad said, "You can do this, m'ijo!" Mr. Hernández told his son that if he really wanted to become an astronaut, he would need to follow a simple, five-ingredient recipe to succeed: 1) decide what you want, 2) recognize how far you are from your goal, 3) draw a road map to get there, 4) prepare yourself with a good education and 5) develop a good work ethic, always giving more than required. In the years to come, José would follow this recipe as he obtained undergraduate and master's degrees in electrical engineering. Adding his own ingredient, perseverance, he applied to NASA's astronaut program eleven times-and was rejected each time! Finally, in 2004, he was selected to be part of the 19th class of US Astronauts. He achieved his dream in 2009 when he served as the flight engineer on the Space Shuttle Discovery on the STS-128 fourteen-day mission to the International Space Station. In From Farmworker to Astronaut, José M. Hernández recollects his parallel journeys, juxtaposing memories of his mission to the space station and childhood aspirations to reach the stars. His story is sure to motivate kids to set goals and reach for their own dreams'—Provided by publisher.
Identifiers: LCCN 2019028873 (print) | LCCN 2019028874 (ebook) | ISBN 9781558858688 (paperback) | ISBN 9781518505430 (ePub) | ISBN 9781518505447 (Kindle edition) | ISBN 9781518505454 (Adobe PDF)
Subjects: LCSH: Hernández, José M., 1962—Juvenile literature. | Astronauts—United States—Biography—Juvenile literature. | Hispanic American astronauts—Biography—Juvenile literature. | Migrant agricultural laborers—California—Biography—Juvenile literature.
Classification: LCC TL789.85.H469 A3 2019b (print) | LCC TL789.85.H469 (ebook) | DDC 629.450092 [B]—dc23
LC record available at https://lccn.loc.gov/2019028873
LC ebook record available at https://lccn.loc.gov/2019028874

Printed in the United States of America
Versa Press, Inc., East Peoria, IL
October 2023–December 2023
5 4 3

This is dedicated to all who dare to dream big and want to make their dream a reality. I wrote this book in the hope that it helps readers reach for their own stars.

Table of Contents

Acknowledgements

One rarely accomplishes worthwhile goals in life by oneself. I certainly had a lot of help and encouragement to reach for the stars on my journey to becoming an astronaut. I would like to start by dedicating this book to the unsung heroes of America, our teachers. I hope they remember my story the moment they doubt whether their efforts make a difference, for if not for the likes of my second-grade teacher, Ms. Young, who convinced my father to set roots here in Stockton, California, I doubt I would have reached my goal of becoming an astronaut. Similarly, I acknowledge my middle school and high school teachers; Mr. Dave Ellis, Ms. Silvia Bello and Mr. Salvador Zendejas, who went above and beyond the call of duty in their teaching efforts; my undergraduate physics professor at the University of the Pacific, Dr. Andrés Rodríguez, who taught me to have self-confidence and always advised me not to psych myself out. I thank my older siblings, Sal, Lety and Gil, who always tutored and guided me through school. My mother for her nurturing yet firm style that kept us academically on track. She always kept the family together regardless of the crisis we faced—believe me, we faced many. I would also like to thank my lovely wife, Adelita, for believing in me and not letting me give up on my dream. To my kids: Julio, Karina, Vanessa, Marisol and Antonio, for making my job of being a good father look easy. To my boss and mentor at Lawrence Livermore National Laboratory, Clint Logan, who not only taught me how to be a good engineer and manager, but also how to be an effective leader. To my daughter, Marisol, for her insightful advice and edits on this book and, finally, to Pops, whose recipe for success is the focus of this book.

Author's Note

This book follows two parallel journeys; from liftoff to landing at NASA Kennedy Space Center, and from my childhood to my lifetime of learning as an engineer, astronaut, father and son. This approach allows the reader, through the eyes of this flight engineer, to not only experience a fourteen-day journey to the International Space Station aboard the Space Shuttle Discovery but also and perhaps more importantly, to understand my journey to becoming an astronaut. The attempt is to encourage the reader to dream big, much like my father did with me when I, as a ten-year-old, shared with him my desire to become an astronaut and to show the reader the tools that are necessary to make that dream a reality. I accomplish this by sharing how I used my father's five-ingredient recipe for success, to which I add a sixth ingredient, and how I discovered that there are three stages to reaching a goal. Though the book may seem like an autobiography, it is an incomplete one as I only include the parts relevant to the recipe and the three stages to reaching a goal. It is my hope that the recipe and the three stages are tools than can be used by the reader to turn their own dream into a reality.

FROM
FARMWORKER
TO
ASTRONAUT

MY PATH TO THE STARS

Getting Ready to Launch

We were scheduled to launch on Tuesday, August 25, 2009, at 1:25 am aboard Space Shuttle Discovery for what was to be a thirteen-day mission to the International Space Station. There is usually a crew of seven astronauts on a space shuttle mission, three in the middeck and four in the flight deck (the section that's called a cockpit on a plane). The three astronauts in the middeck are basically sacks of potatoes during the first eight and a half minutes of powered space flight because they don't have any flight operation responsibilities. However, once they are in space they have the best job of all. They are the ones who perform the extra-vehicular activities (EVA's), better known as spacewalks.

I was part of the flight deck crew and served as the engineer, also known as Mission Specialist 2 (MS-2). I had the best seat in the house during both the launch and the landing operations because I sat in the middle, behind the commander and the pilot. This gave me a panoramic view of the outside and of all the displays that both the commander and the pilot utilized during

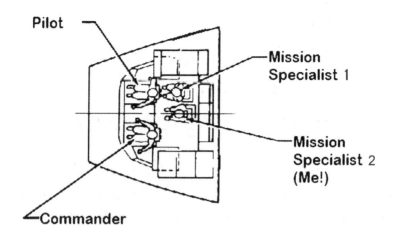

Pilot

Mission
Specialist 1

Mission
Specialist 2
(Me!)

Commander

launch and landing. Of course, we were *all* very busy during launch and landing operations.

The final two weeks of training for our mission took us right into quarantine, a period of isolation that prevents astronauts from getting sick in space. We started our quarantine at Johnson Space Center in Houston, Texas. After the first two weeks of quarantine we flew NASA T-38 jets from Ellington Field in Houston to the Kennedy Space Center in Florida, and continued our quarantine in the crew quarters there.

Before landing at Kennedy, we did a flyby of the launch pad complex, where we were able to see Space Shuttle Discovery in its vertical launch position. Discovery was attached to a large, orange external tank and two solid white rocket boosters. The large, orange tank was made up of two smaller tanks, one containing more than 395,000 gallons of cryogenic (super-chilled) liquid hydrogen fuel and the other with more than 146,000 gallons of super-chilled liquid oxygen that served as an oxidizer and allowed the burning fuel to combust. At liftoff, these tanks would feed the three main shuttle engines at a combined rate of almost 65,000 gallons per minute. The space shuttle would need the engines' 37-million horsepower to lift off and to make our journey to the International Space Station.

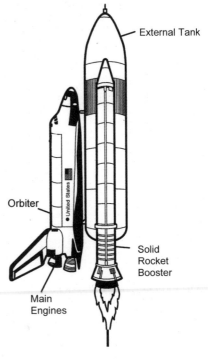

External Tank

Orbiter

Main Engines

Solid Rocket Booster

The station travels in a set path around the earth called an orbit, just like the moon. These objects in orbit are called satellites. Without gravity, an Earth-orbiting satellite would go off into space. Like a baseball hit by a bat, the satellite has a tendency to move in a straight line, but the tug of gravity is always pulling it back. This effect of gravity is what makes the space station and the moon travel in an orbit. Our mission was to not only travel beyond the Earth's atmosphere and enter orbit, but to navigate to the International Space Station and dock there.

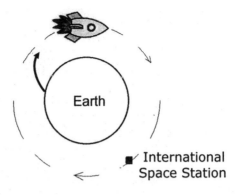

Seeing the shuttle in its upright position and fully stacked with the tank and solid rocket boosters was so exciting. Every time I saw the launch pad and the shuttle, I was impressed by its size. The pad was a quarter mile square and the steel structure the shuttle launched from measured almost two hundred feet in the air. In less than a week, this would be our ride into space! I saw the orbiter access arm that we would use to enter the shuttle and the Emergency Egress Slidewire Baskets. The sets of seven baskets were designed to provide the flight and the closeout crews a quick exit off the launch pad in the event of an emergency.

Ever since a fire in the cockpit killed three astronauts before liftoff during the Apollo 1 mission in 1967, NASA has taken launch safety very seriously. We had practiced this during our three-day launch pad escape training exercises. When the baskets were released, they descended quickly down a 1,200-foot slide wire away from the launch pad, taking us to the safety of a reinforced bunker.

While we were in quarantine, anyone who needed to meet with us, including our spouses, had to be checked by a flight surgeon to ensure they were completely healthy. During the quarantine period, we continued to train to stay proficient and confident.

Although our launch date was Tuesday, August 25, 2009, we knew that mostly everything would occur on the day before: Monday, August 24. This was because the actual launch time was to be at 1:36:05 in the morning on Tuesday. Therefore, when we woke up that Monday, we eagerly posed for a photo of what we thought would be our "last breakfast before going to space" and had a traditional breakfast of steak and scrambled eggs.

Part of the day's activities included a weather briefing; according to my notes, we had a 20% chance that the weather would cause a launch delay. My notes also indicated that lightning, common for that time of year in Florida, would be present but most likely not within a ten-mile radius of the launch pad complex. It was all systems go.

The crew usually entered the space shuttle a good four hours before the launch, which meant we would also enjoy dinner in our crew quarters. For dinner, we were allowed to order anything we wanted: steak, burgers or seafood. The folks at crew quarters took very good care of us, and the food they prepared was excellent. And I know a lot about good food, my wife at the time owned and operated a Mexican restaurant called Tierra Luna Grill in Clear Lake City near NASA.

I was a little anxious before this first mission. I had heard stories of "space adaptation syndrome," typically referred to as space sickness, a condition experienced by about half of all space travelers in a mild form, and in a more severe form by about ten percent of them. It occurs during the process of adapting to weightlessness. It is related to motion sickness, and symptoms usually subside within two to four days in space. I did not want to chance getting sick, so I ordered a light dinner: a bland baked potato and a couple of dry biscuits.

After dinner and a few more preparatory meetings, I went to my bedroom in the crew quarters to retrieve my landing bag, which contained my passport and the civilian clothes that I would wear once we landed from our space mission. The passport was necessary in case of an emergency landing at one of the designated sites in Europe or any other place in the world. If such a landing occurred, our support personnel would fly to that location to give us our passports, which we would need to exit the country where we landed and to re-enter the United States. I could not help but notice how empty my bedroom looked now that all my family pictures were packed away and ready to go to space with me.

Finally, it was time for us to go next door to the Operations and Checkout Building to suit up. This was the last step before we traveled aboard the Astronaut Transfer Van to make the twenty-minute drive from

Operations and Checkout to the launch pad. Also known as the Astrovan, the vehicle was basically a modified, stainless-steel vintage Airstream RV. We astronauts had pleaded with NASA not to replace the Astrovan, because many astronauts had traveled the nine miles to the launch pad in that same van before us, and we wanted to keep the tradition alive.

Every astronaut that travels to space is allowed a "personal preference kit" in which they place the belongings that will travel into space with them. The contents of the kit are limited to twenty separate items totaling no more than 1.5 pounds. The contents have to fit in a NASA-issued bag that measures 5" x 8" x 2". There is barely enough space for a wedding ring, a kid's necklace and a watch.

Fortunately for me, before I had been assigned to this mission, I was given a technical assignment that consisted of being on a four-person astronaut team known as the "astronaut support personnel." The team, also nicknamed Cape Crusader, would travel from Houston to Kennedy a few days before each launch and spend the days and evenings inside the space shuttle prepping, testing and calibrating all the flight-related hardware. On launch day, the lead Cape Crusader would serve as the seventh person of the seven-person closeout crew.

In this closeout crew team, there was always one active astronaut like me. The closeout crew helped the astronauts strap into the shuttle module and took care of any other last-minute needs. Ultimately, the crew would seal the access hatch once all the astronauts were strapped into their launch seats. This team consists of two suit technicians from Johnson Space Center, three technicians from Kennedy, a NASA-quality inspector and the lead Cape Crusader. I was able to participate in six of these launches as a Cape Crusader and was the lead in my last two launches. This allowed me to develop a great relationship with the closeout crew.

I have to confess that I really wanted to bring additional items into space with me. These items included the pictures of my family I had in my bedroom at crew quarters; a small flag of my favorite football team, the Oakland Raiders; a small Mexican flag I planned to present to the president of Mexico and a San Diego Chargers hat. This was because the Spanos family, who were from my hometown of Stockton, California, owned the Chargers. I talked to my closeout crewmembers about the additional items I wanted to bring into space and one of them asked me to leave the items outside my bedroom before the launch. With a wink and a nudge, he let me know that these items would "conveniently" find their way into the saddlebag next to my seat, where all my flight manuals were kept.

I grabbed my landing bag and went into the suit room, where some of my crewmates had already gathered. The suit room had seven stations, each with a seat that resembled a reclining chair. As we entered, we were given an adult diaper and a blue Liquid Cooling and Ventilation Garment known as the LCVG. To me, the LCVG resembled a Spiderman suit; it was made of tight-fitting elastic fabric, with flexible tubing sewn onto the fabric. Because of its tight-fitting

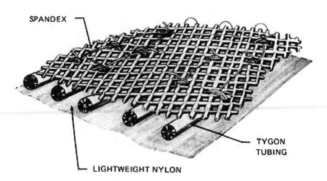

SPANDEX

TYGON TUBING

LIGHTWEIGHT NYLON

nature, the tubing came in very close contact with our skin and provided excellent cooling. For this to occur, it had inlet and outlet hoses that allowed the cool water to enter and circulate throughout the body. After circulating, the now warmer water exited for re-cooling via a portable heat exchanger or the shuttle's cooling system. Controlling the cool water flow rate allowed the wearer to adjust to a comfortable setting. I immediately went back to my bedroom and changed into the diaper and the LCVG. The diaper was highly recommended because it could be up to five or six hours before you were allowed to remove the suit. The wait could be even longer, as we were about to find out, if the flight launch time was postponed.

I went back to the suit room and was immediately assisted into the Launch Entry Suit (LES), commonly referred to as the "pumpkin suit" because of its bright orange color. The LES was a pressurized suit that space shuttle crews used for the ascent and entry portions of flight. This LES, along with a sealed helmet, allowed a pressurized environment to exist and was a safety feature that protected each crewmember in the event the cabin experienced depressurization during the high-altitude portion of the flight. Human beings are adapted to the air pressure on earth and cannot breathe or maintain their body temperature under different conditions. If the cabin lost pressure, my pumpkin suit and my Spiderman liquid cooling suit would allow me to breathe and would keep my blood from boiling! Once the suit technicians dressed us, attached the gloves and helmet and connected us to a portable heat exchanger, they performed suit leak tests, a process that could take up to two hours—we did all of this in a diaper.

After being suited up, we were almost ready to head to the launch pad. But we had to wait for Commander Rick "CJ" Sturckow to perform an astronaut ritual: he played cards with the branch chief. A combination of blackjack and five-card poker, the game had been played since the first American spaceflights, when the first two-man crews flew. The tradition was

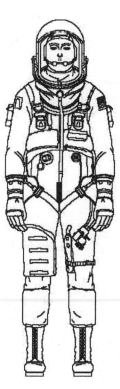

that the mission commander had to play until he or she lost the hand.

After CJ finally lost, we headed toward the elevator and were greeted by technicians, fellow astronauts and crew quarters personnel. Coming out of the elevator, the area was cordoned off and cleared of people, thus providing a clear path to the brightly lit Astrovan parked outside the building. As we walked to the van, about two hundred Kennedy Space Center employees cheered us on and took our pictures. It was a relief to be connected to the portable heat exchanger coolers; without them, wearing a heavy space suit in August in Florida in our vintage Astrovan would have been far from comfortable. We settled in for the twenty-minute ride to launch pad 39A. At the launch pad, we each carried our portable coolers and headed toward one of the launch tower elevators that would take us to Space Shuttle Discovery.

We took the elevator in groups of four to the 195-foot level and congregated in an area between the entrance of the access arm and the baskets that allowed the flight and closeout crews to exit the launch pad quickly in an emergency. The Commander,

Pilot and Mission Specialist-1 were strapped into the flight deck before me and the three other astronauts in the mid-deck. When I finally got the call to board, I carefully went in through the hatch, crawled into the flight deck and took my seat. It was not as easy as it sounds: the very bulky, ninety-pound pumpkin LES suit made even simple move-

ments in a small space with hundreds of switches quite a challenge. As soon as I was seated, a closeout crewmember installed my gloves and helmet and connected my suit to oxygen and the LCVG to water.

The final step before they left us was for me to perform a communications check. Next, the closeout crew looked around to make sure all unnecessary items were removed from the vehicle. After that, they exited, closed the hatch and took the elevator down. They would be the first responders in the event of an emergency.

We were now a good two hours and forty-five minutes from launch. We performed our communications checks with the Launch Control Center director and staff; this was followed by an air-to-ground voice check with Mission Control Center back in Houston. While we waited to launch, I started to feel a bit more comfortable and at ease. These long pauses allowed us to gather our thoughts so we could focus on the next steps, such as checking cabin leaks, air-to-ground communication, cabin pressure and to ensure the backup flight computer was operational. After these steps were completed, we had to wait about an hour for launch. This wait period is known as the "L Minus 20-Minute" hold. I knew we had about ten to fifteen minutes before the clock would once again resume its countdown sequence, with another scheduled hold at launch minus nine minutes. The hold at minus twenty was a built-in delay to allow for the launch director to conduct final briefings for our team and for the guidance folks to complete the preflight alignments that would keep us on the desired trajectory throughout the mission.

As soon as the twenty-minute hold began, I started to notice raindrops hitting our windshield. They seemed more like a mist, so I thought nothing of it. Soon we were out of the minus-twenty hold and the clock once again began counting down. At this point, our flight computers, including the backup flight computer were being loaded with the first operational sequence known as OPS1. This brought us to the minus nine-minute hold.

I could not help but notice that the frequency and size of those drops hitting our front windshield had dramatically increased and that there were flashes of lightning in the distance. As we waited, I felt sorry for the hundred or so of my invited guests, including my immediate family, who were a mere four miles away and were also exposed to the weather. Later, I would learn that they did not receive one drop of rain, that it was only sprinkling around the launch pad.

A few moments into the hold, the launch director indicated they were observing the weather and for us to standby. It was now a waiting game, with the launch window and the weather being the two variables.

CHAPTER 2

L Minus 9-Minutes and Holding

During the L minus 9-minute hold, I begin to think about my long journey from stargazer to astronaut in the flight deck of a space shuttle that was waiting to launch. Ever since I could remember, I considered myself an adventurer and an explorer. This was because of my childhood. We were migrant farmworkers from La Piedad, Michoacán, Mexico. To be more precise, we were from an unincorporated village known as Ticuitaco, near the city of La Piedad. We lived a nomadic life that brought us to several locations in the United States and Mexico throughout the year.

However, my story begins well before I was born. It begins when my father was fifteen years old. Pops, as my siblings and I called him, came from a family of twelve kids. He was the fourth oldest. Those days in rural Mexico, if you were a boy, you grew up and went to school up to the third grade. After that, you were considered old enough and strong enough to help your father and his ox work the fields of corn, garbanzo beans and alfalfa. If you were a girl, you also went to school, usually up to the third grade, and then helped your mother with the household chores. This included shucking corn and removing it from the cob to allow it to dry, feeding and cleaning the pigs and feeding the chickens, turkeys and the one or two cows each household owned. When you reached the age of fourteen or fifteen, it was expected that you would be engaged to be married to one of the local boys.

After a rainless season when Pops was fifteen, he decided to do what many of the young men were doing to help their struggling families: go north to California and look for work. The type of work the young men from the state of Michoacán were doing in California was the only work they knew how to do: farm labor, especially if, like Pops, they were undocumented and in the country without the government's permission. In short, his job was to pick whichever fruits or vegetables were in season. The working conditions were poor, but the young men were paid in American dollars, currency that went a lot further than *pesos* did back home. As the years went by, my father continued to make his annual trip to California and returned home each year for the winter.

When Pops came home for the Christmas holiday after his third harvest season in California, he met my mother. He was eighteen, and she was almost fourteen years old. As Mom explains it, it was love at first sight. Their courtship began just days after she met him. Three months later both my grandfather and a priest accompanied my father to Mom's house to ask for her hand in marriage. The agreement was that Pops would go back to California to work and return with enough money to host the wedding. Everything went as planned, they got married when Pops was nineteen and my mother was almost fifteen.

After the wedding, Pops initially left my mother behind with my paternal grandparents, José (my namesake) and Cleotilde Hernández. Soon after, Pops applied for and received permanent resident status in the United States. Now that he could come and go as he pleased, he quickly applied on Mom's behalf for her residency status. When Mom received her status, Pops and Mom decided that she would accompany him on his yearly trips to California.

Mom and Pops eventually had four children: three boys and one girl. Salvador Jr. is the oldest, followed by my sister Leticia, then my brother Gil and finally me. My parents wanted to have more children, but after Mom miscarried, the doctor recommended she not have any more kids.

I was born in the month of August, which was peak harvest. My parents followed the harvest, starting in southern California and working their way north. I was born at our last stop of the season in the San Joaquin General Hospital French Camp, next to the city where we lived at that time, Stockton, California. My brother who is closest in age to me, Gil, was born in September, before the family returned to Mexico. However, my two oldest siblings, Sal Jr., or Chava as we call him, and our sister Leticia, or Lety, were born in the winter months in my parents' homeland. Today, I kid with Chava and Lety because, even though they are now naturalized US citizens, I tease them of the US Constitution, of how I could one day be elected president of the United States while they could not.

The chatter on the shuttle communication system brought me back to reality. The launch director announced that soon we would have to make a Go-No-Go decision. The rain had not let up and there were flashes of lightning in the dark sky above. A few minutes later, the launch director notified our commander that the mission was canceled for that evening.

Extremely disappointed, we began the process of egressing from the Space Shuttle Discovery. Being a numbers guy, I calculated that each canceled mission cost over $1.2 million dollars. The high price was due to the cost of personnel, as well as the evaporation of super-chilled liquid hydrogen and liquid oxygen propellants stored in the external tank. Although the vast majority of this fuel could be recycled if a liftoff was canceled, some of it would boil away, about half a million dollars' worth. The other $700,000 would be used on the workforce who would spend hours making the shuttle safe and preparing for another launch attempt. The next launch attempt was scheduled for Wednesday, August 26 at 1:10 am, a mere 23 hours and 34 minutes later.

Back at crew quarters, we had a debrief meeting and were told why the launch had been scrubbed. To no one's surprise, precipitation and lightning were the culprits. Once the meeting ended, I went into the kitchen and made myself a fully loaded ham sandwich, grabbed a bag of chips and a can of soda and ate like there was no tomorrow. When I finished my meal, I called my wife, who was back at the hotel trying to get the kids to sleep. I gave her a blow-by-blow description of our launch attempt, wished her a good night and headed to bed. What a day!

As I lay in bed, I was still so pumped up that it was hard to fall asleep. My thoughts went back to my childhood. I wondered, what was the earliest event in my life that I could remember? Surprisingly, I was able to recollect my days as a kindergartner. I still remember when we lived near Modesto, California. The Central Valley of California was always our family's last stop as we followed the harvest north. At that time, we lived in a small farmhouse at the end of a dirt road the farmer provided for Pops and my two uncles, who also worked on the farm and tended to the tomatoes, sugar beets and corn crops. I grew up with them, Tío Raúl and Tío

Roberto. Tío Raúl was still single and Tío Roberto had not yet brought his family to California. It was like growing up with three hard-working father figures. The farmer must have loved the idea of having three farm hands living in his one farmhouse, as opposed to just one member of the family working on the farm, as Pops often said.

I recalled that on the first day of school, a new and shiny yellow bus had stopped for us at the entrance to our dirt road. We were about 800 yards from the paved road, and the bus was now waiting patiently with its doors open. When I got in I smelled that new bus smell. And with my three siblings, we passed the occupied seats and tried not to notice the stares of our fellow passengers. We found seats together toward the back of the bus. My brothers and sister looked calm and collected. I, on the other hand, was full of fear. It was fear of the unknown. I did not really understand the English language. My only friends were my siblings, and my parents always had the television set on Spanish programming, so there had been little opportunity to learn English. This nervousness, coupled with the fact that the bus was now navigating through curves and making sharp turns, soon created the perfect environment for me to feel sick.

When we got to the school, I remember rushing off the bus so I could take a deep breath of fresh air. This immediately made me feel better. Chava took me to my classroom. He explained that I would get out earlier than he would, and that I would need to take the bus by myself, then walk down the dirt road home. The first day of school was complete chaos. I had a hard time understanding the teacher, but I quickly learned to wait for my classmates to begin each activity so that I could follow along. My favorite part of being in kindergarten was the cookie, milk and nap.

Soon, I developed a routine in school and was proud that when my teacher said, "Students, please grab your pencil" or "Students, please grab your crayons," I actually knew what she meant. I also looked forward to coming home on the bus. Usually, Pops or one of my uncles, whoever drove the tractor that day, would wait for me where our dirt road met the blacktop to give me a ride to the farmhouse. Inside the house, Mom was always ready to give me something to eat before I was allowed to go outside and play by myself and patiently wait for my siblings to arrive from school.

As the night wore on and the effects of the adrenaline subsided, I fell into a deep sleep. I woke up the next morning, Tuesday, August 25, to the smell of bacon being cooked in the kitchen. I quickly showered and dressed and met some of the crew already putting in their orders for breakfast.

As the rest of the team arrived, CJ gave us an update: "Crew, everything stays the same. We will be doing everything we did yesterday, except that things will be shifted about twenty minutes or so earlier."

This one-day delay had caused our launch window to slip by about twenty minutes; the new time required that we catch up to reach the same orbit as the International Space Station to dock there.

As the day wore on, we found out that instead of the 80% go for launch we had the previous night, our odds had fallen to 70% for launch. *Geez,* I thought, *I hope we don't get another weather delay!* But that's August in Florida: thunderstorms and rain. Remembering how hungry I had been the previous night, I decided to eat a hearty lunch and dinner. In fact, I even dressed my baked potato with sour cream, bacon bits and chives. I also put butter on my warm biscuits. Soon after dinner, it was time once again to go to the suit room, grab the adult-sized diaper, LCVG and change.

Entering the suit room in my blue Spiderman outfit, I once again went to my station, where the suit technician proceeded to dress me into the orange LES. Coolant loop installed? Check. Gloves installed? Check. Helmet installed? Check. Next, we did our communications and pressure leak test checks. Everything was going smoothly. I saw my crewmates finish up as well. Then I saw some of the senior staff huddled together at the commander's station. *This can't be good,* I thought.

Sure enough: the commander approached and said, "Crew, this mission is being delayed again. We don't have a new launch date, but standby."

One of us asked, "Why the delay?"

"Apparently," he said, "a faulty LH2 fuel valve sensor or valve needs to be replaced. They should have more information for us later tonight."

NASA, to my relief, takes safety very seriously and for good reason too. One only has to go back to 2003 when we lost the Space Shuttle Columbia and its crew during re-entry. This was due to the apparent damage caused to the thermal protection system on the wing leading edge by the impact of insulating foam from the external tank during its 8 ½ minutes of powered flight into space. In 1986 we lost the Challenger and its crew 73 seconds into the flight due to an O-ring failure and in 1967 the Apollo 1 crew was lost during a pre-flight test. Each of these failures reminds us that going into space is not routine, and hence every precaution needs to be taken to ensure the safety of the crew and success of the mission.

Later that evening we found out that it was the sensors that had not detected the closure of the valve. After draining the external tank, tests were conducted on the valves and, despite them working as designed, it was decided that the third launch opportunity would be on Friday, August 28, at 23:59 EDT.

Some of the guests I had invited to watch the launch had to return home to work or school. On the other hand, some simply could not afford to change their flights or the cost of additional nights at their hotel. My immediate family, however, was there to stick it out until Space Shuttle Discovery finally launched.

As Tuesday evening approached, I decided to hit the rack earlier than normal. It had been a busy couple of days. As I got ready for bed and lay down to rest my eyes for a while, I once again started to think about my childhood.

CHAPTER 3

A Teacher's Visit

By the time I entered first grade I understood some English, I was learning a lot more and school was not as scary. I was now in school full-time and on the same schedule as my siblings. But there were other challenges.

Pops was always looking for jobs because the farm where he worked did not offer stable work, and we had to move around a lot. As a result, we attended two or three schools a year. Our school year in California actually began in February because we would be in Mexico until then. Pops would load us four kids and Mom into the car to make the two-day trip back to Southern California. We would be cramped in the back seat of our sedan all the way from Mexico.

Because I was the youngest and claimed to get car sick, I was allowed to have a window seat most of the way. I'd pass the time during the long ride pretending to be an explorer on a trip to the unknown. This was more realistic at night, when all I could see were the stars and moon. During those trips, the moon and stars called out to me.

On these trips through California, Mom always had a basket packed with *tortas*—sandwiches made with

French bread rolls and ham, beans, sour cream, lettuce, tomatoes and cheese. She usually added slices of pickled *jalapeño* peppers for the adults. We had these with soda or water.

"Don't drink too much," Pops would say, "because I don't want to make a lot of stops for bathroom breaks."

The second meal during the trip was usually tacos made of beans, potatoes and deep fried beef or pork. They were crunchy when you bit into them. If we were traveling south to Mexico, the menu had a third item: soup. Pops always made sure he loaded several loaves of Wonder bread and plenty of cans of Campbell's chicken noodle soup. We'd eat these when we ran out of *tacos* and *tortas*. When Pops sensed we were getting hungry, he would pull over to the side of the road, open the hood of the car and carefully place three or four cans of soup on top of the engine manifold. Then he'd close the hood and continue to drive. About thirty minutes later, he would stop again, pull out the cans, open them and pour the warm soup into cups. We'd each get one along with a plastic spoon and three slices of bread. Then he'd quickly resume the drive.

Pops would drive well into the night and pull over to the side of the road only when he was completely exhausted, which was usually around one or two in the morning. I remember being awakened a few hours later when Pops started the engine. And away we went again.

Even though Mom and Pops had not gone beyond the third grade at school, they were united in the goal of getting us kids a formal education at a school and not just in the fields where we were learning so much about life. They did not know where that additional education would take us, but they were sure it would allow us to have more opportunities than farm work.

I remember working in the fields when we were not in school on the weekends. Us kids were awakened at about 4:30 in the morning and hastily dressed to join Mom and Pops for a day of work in the strawberry fields near the Ontario-Chino areas of southern California. Work usually started at daybreak and ended around 2:00 pm. We were paid according to how many boxes of strawberries we picked.

Mom would allow me to stay in the car a little longer than the rest because I was the youngest, but Pops didn't want her to treat me like a baby. He told her, if I could walk, I could also pick strawberries! It was hard work; you had to crouch to pick the berries, and your legs would feel like they were going to fall asleep. When you stood up blood would rush to your legs and make you feel woozy. I was too young and slow to have my own row to pick. I would shadow my mom and pick from her row. That's how I became the designated go-for: go for water, go for the tacos in the car, go for the sodas. I welcomed the role because anything was better than picking strawberries!

Near the city of Salinas in central California, Mom and Pops worked harvesting lettuce in early spring. On weekends, Mom and Dad would still take us to the fields, but we had to wait in the car until it was warm enough to go outside and play. The lettuce harvest involved lots of moving machinery in the field, and kids were not allowed for safety reasons. This machinery included a big, long trailer-like contraption that covers over 12 rows of lettuce and moves sideways along the rows. Behind this trailer contraption were about 12 people, usually men, picking the iceberg lettuce and tossing it onto a moving conveyer belt. On this belt they sort, rinse, bag and pack the lettuce in boxes. These boxes when full are loaded onto another conveyor belt that extends out to a flatbed trailer truck that is following from behind. Here workers swiftly but carefully load the boxes on the flatbed trailers where they seal and label and neatly stack the boxes. When full, another empty trailer truck moves into position while the loaded truck drives off to the refrigerated distribution center. The picking of other types of lettuce like Romaine and Baby Romaine are pretty similar with a few differences, such as Baby Romaine are not individually bagged but put into a box that has a plastic bag liner.

Pops would always park the car under a large stand of trees that provided plenty of shade and protection from the winds that were strong in that area. As we waited for our parents, we would play hide-and-seek, tag or hopscotch. Time seemed to fly by. Before we knew it, Mom and Pops would show up, tired but happy to see we had not called unwanted attention to ourselves. After about a month or two there, we would pack our things up and drive a few hours north to the Stockton-Modesto-Tracy area in the Central Valley. It was there that we would spend five to six months. My parents would work picking a variety of fruits and vegetables. We would of course join them on weekends and seven days a week during the summer. We would arrive into the Stockton area late in April and would not leave for Mexico until the end of the harvest, which was in the early part of November. It was there that we finished one school year and began another.

The buzzer of my alarm in the bedroom of crew quarters woke me up from my deep sleep. I had set it for 6:30 in the morning. It was Wednesday, August 26, 2009. I woke up more relaxed than I had been the day before, because I knew that all we had scheduled were meetings regarding the status of Discovery and the faulty fuel valve sensor. I had set the alarm to go off a little earlier than normal so that I could have a chance to go out for a five-mile run. Although crew quarters had a gym with a couple of treadmills and stationary bicycles, I much preferred running outdoors. Something about seeing the scenery change made me feel that a run outside was a better workout than a run on a treadmill. After my workout and a quick shower, I met some of my crewmates for breakfast. Our commander was already in meetings being briefed on the status of the work, and we soon joined him. After dinner that night, our commander selected a movie together as a crew. He was a fan of westerns and Paul Newman so he chose "Cool Hand Luke." The most memorable quote of the movie was, "What we have here is a failure to communicate." I can only guess that the commander wanted us to not only enjoy a movie but also impress upon us that communication as a crew was of utmost importance and that failing to do so effectively could be deadly. *Certainly a good lesson,* I thought.

After the movie, we turned in for the night. As I lay in bed, I thought about my childhood again. This time, I remembered my family's last stop of the year in our journey north, in Stockton, California.

It was June, and the school year was almost finished. I was excited and proud of myself that I could understand almost everything the teacher said and that I was going to be a second-grader. My classmates were elated because summer vacation was nearly upon us, but I was not so excited because I knew we would work in the fields every day of the week.

In late April, when we arrived in Stockton, cucumbers were the first crop to come into season. Crews of about forty people picked several fields per day. One picker would claim a row of cucumber plants, go along the row standing but bending his or her back and picking as quickly as possible, filling and dragging a metal bucket along. When the bucket was full, the worker had to pick it up and make a fast dash down to the end of the row, where there was a tractor hauling four wooden bins on a trailer. The farmworker then poured the bucket of cucumbers into one of the bins. After another worker on the trailer made sure the picker had not included vines from the cucumber plant, or oversized or over-ripe cucumbers, the worker would give the picker a chip that was worth fifty cents. It was a simple concept, the harder you worked, the more buckets you picked and the more money you earned.

The work was back-breaking. It was cold and muddy in the early hours of the day, and hot and steamy as the day wore on. One of the things you always wanted to avoid was to step on an oversized or over-ripe cucumber. If you did, the rotten thing would release a foul stench that would almost make you vomit!

The fields were harvested about every three days. Once we picked it, the field was immediately irrigated and this short timespan between harvesting and irrigating did not allow the field to dry. This meant that the fields were still wet in the morning, and that made our pants damp and muddy. Our pants would eventually dry in the hot sun. The badge of honor among the Hernández kids was not who picked the most buckets of cucumbers, but rather who could carefully take their jeans off and stand them up by themselves once we were home! I would win this competition because in the mornings, when no one was looking and I was already warm from picking several buckets of cucumbers, I would roll on the ground in the middle of the row to get the mud all over my pants. By end of the day, my dry pants were the stiffest of them all!

After cucumber season we hoed sugar beets. Then we picked cherries, onions and peaches from the orchards. Next, it was green tomatoes for market. We ended the harvest with the grape season.

My alarm buzzed and woke me up from a restful night of sleep. I once again had set it for 6:30 in the morning. It was Thursday, August 27, 2009. I felt a bit tired, probably from yesterday's run, or perhaps because I had thought so much about the fieldwork I did as a child. Regardless, I decided to go out for one last five-mile run before our mission. *One more day before we go into space!* I thought.

The day would be pretty much a repeat of yesterday: have a nice breakfast, meetings all morning, lunch, more meetings, dinner and a movie. We were still in quarantine and were not allowed to wander around the base (unless you went out for a jog), much less go into town. After all that, I found myself in bed reminiscing about my family's life as migrant workers.

It was the end of summer 1969, and a summer of hard work. I started the second grade at Fillmore Elementary School on the east side of Stockton—a little more than a mile from the house we rented. In those days, one was expected to walk if the school was only a mile or so away. Nowadays, I think parents would get arrested for child endangerment if we made our kids walk a mile to school! Different times, I guess.

The second grade was exciting. I had a new teacher, Ms. Young, who was a young, beautiful Asian-American woman with a lot of enthusiasm. She quickly noticed that I struggled with English and spent a lot of her free time making sure I understood the lessons.

"Well, young man, what's your favorite subject?" Ms. Young asked.

"Math," I said with enthusiasm. "It's easy for me. And, 1+3=4 is the same in Spanish as it is in English."

"Hmm . . . what else?"

"Well, I love to stare at the stars and moon at night . . . and especially at dawn."

"At dawn? What are you doing up at dawn?"

"Uh . . . that's when we go to work in the fields. My father drives us and, when we get there, I'm the first to get out of the car and allow my eyes to adapt to the dark. I get about five to ten minutes to look at the stars. And if I'm lucky, I sometimes see a falling star!"

One day before the bell rang for us to go home, Ms. Young called me to her desk and handed me a large hardback book. "This is for you," she said. "Since you like to gaze at the stars, I figured you would like a book on astronomy."

Eagerly, I paged through the pictures of planets and galaxies in the book.

"The book is for you to keep, José, but the only promise you have to make to me is that you read it."

"¡Sí, gracias!" I replied.

That day, I went straight home. After I finished my homework, I dove into my new book: *The Sun, the Moon and the Stars*. I must have read it a couple of hundred times over the next few years! Our family moved many times and I lost track of my book, but it pointed my life in the right direction.

One early November day as we woke up and started to get ready to go to school, Pops made his annual announcement: "*Muchachos*, we will be going back to Mexico next week. Please tell your teachers to prepare three months of homework."

Mom and Pops believed in education—we were always in school while we were in California—but they knew that putting us in school in Mexico would confuse us and make it harder for us to learn English. In addition, whatever time we had in school there would be interrupted by the Christmas and Three Kings holidays. So, my parents made us study regularly. Every Monday through Friday while we were in Mexico, Mom would wake us up early, give us a cup of hot chocolate and a piece of French bread or *pan dulce*, then from 8:00 in the morning to noon she supervised us from afar to ensure we did our homework. Our work may have had chocolate stains, but Mom would make sure we finished the three months of assignments our teachers in California had given us. After Pops' announcement that morning, I got ready for school and headed out the door with Chava, Gil and Lety. When I got to my second-grade classroom, well before everyone was settled in their desks, I went up to Ms. Young and told her I would be leaving for Mexico.

Her happy expression turned serious. She thought a bit and then said, "You tell your parents that I will pay them a visit late this afternoon."

I nodded my head. As soon as school was over, I ran home to tell my parents the important message! I was yelling in my thoughts, "The teacher is coming, the teacher is coming!" I felt like Paul Revere delivering the message of "The British are coming, the British are coming!"

When I got home, I first ran into Pops in the living room and gave him the news. Pops at the time was a man of few words and very strict with us. He took what I call "the tough love approach" and was always quick to jump to conclusions, often imagining the worst. Hence, he did not let me finish. He immediately stood up, his face flushed red with anger.

"What happened?" he growled. He assumed the teacher was coming to complain about my behavior.

I took a few steps backwards and said that it was about our trip to Mexico.

"Well, you better be right, or else the punishment is going to be severe!"

Phew, close call!

Next, I went to the kitchen to tell Mom about Ms. Young's visit. Mom was the complete opposite of Pops. She was very caring. After school, she would seat us down at the kitchen table to feed us beans and rice with freshly made tortillas while she ensured we started and finished our homework. She was nurturing yet firm, as we were not allowed to get up and go play outside until the homework was completely done. Upon giving her the news about Ms. Young's visit, she was more concerned about the condition the house was in and how we needed to get it ready. Instead of telling us to start our homework, she began to give orders.

"Chava, you pick up the living room. Gil, you clean up the bathroom. Lety, you clean up the kitchen while I cook. And Pepito (a term of endearment for me), you clean up both bedrooms."

Okay, the living room, kitchen and bathroom I understood, but the bedrooms? *There was no way Ms. Young was going to go into our bedrooms, so why clean them?* I thought. Well, I did not dare to challenge my mom and dutifully went about to put both bedrooms in nice, neat order.

Keeping to her word, Ms. Young arrived late that afternoon. After an exchange of pleasantries, Mom asked the whole family and Ms. Young to join her in the kitchen. My whole family sat down around the dinner table: Pops and Mom opposite me, my siblings sitting on to the sides of my parents and Ms. Young sitting next to me on my right. Mom had prepared a quick feast. I did my best to keep the conversation flowing through dinner. It was hard because Mom and Pops only spoke Spanish and Ms. Young only English. There were many uncomfortable pauses. The first ended when Ms. Young praised the food Mom had prepared. Then came a longer one, so I decided to throw my two cents in and jump-start a conversation.

"Ms. Young . . . "

"Yes, José . . . ?" she responded.

"You ought to come over more often!"

Everyone around the table laughed or giggled. Everyone except Pops! Things were taking a very serious turn. Pops looked at us kids and gave us what we called "the look." It meant that he would deal with us after the company had left. We finished our meal and Pops invited Ms. Young to the living room, where Mom offered coffee. I, too, was invited to the living room, not only because Ms. Young was my teacher, but also because I would serve as the official translator.

Ms. Young started in. "Mr. and Mrs. Hernández, thank you so much for the lovely dinner. It was delicious. But I did not come to eat. I'm here to talk about your children's education."

Immediately, Pops pepped up and asked, "Are our kids misbehaving, Ms. Young?"

Ms. Young sensed Pops' imagination running wild and put him at ease. "No, Mr. Hernández. In fact, I spoke to all of their teachers, who said they are all well-behaved and are very good students. I have the pleasure of having had most of them in my class for second grade. They are all very bright."

Both Pops and Mom were relieved to hear this report.

"But . . . I am truly concerned about the nomadic lifestyle your family is living."

"¿Nómadas?" Pops asked, puzzled.

"Yes. Your children have attended three different schools in one year!"

Pops got really defensive and shot back, "Even though my wife and I only have a third-grade education, we value education more than anything. Yes, we do move around to look for work, but I assure you that we always move on weekends and the kids don't miss a single day of school."

Ms. Young then fired back, "But you go back to Mexico and they miss a lot of school!"

"True," Pops said, "but they take homework."

As I translated for them, I could sense Ms. Young's frustration because she clearly was not getting her message through to Pops. In his eyes, Pops was providing us with an education, nevermind that we got it from three different schools during the school year and with three months of homeschooling in between!

Ms. Young paused for a moment, then quickly perked up and faced Pops again. "Okay, I see that I am not making myself clear, but let me give you an example."

"Sure," Pops said.

"I can see you're a good father," Ms. Young started. "And you know a lot about farm work . . . how to care for plants and trees."

"Well, yes . . . I've spent my whole life doing field work."

"Exactly," said Ms. Young. "Then perhaps you can help me with the following problem?"

"Okay, shoot," Pops said.

"If I give you four small fruit trees in containers and I ask you to find the most fertile ground around this area and dig four holes to plant these trees there . . . And I ask you to ensure they have all the care they need, including enough water and fertilizer to keep them healthy . . . "

"Okay," Pops answered with a quizzical look on his face.

"Then in three months, I want you to find another piece of fertile land and dig four more holes and transplant those four trees. Again, I need you to ensure they are watered and fertilized and given the best care."

"Okay," Pops agreed once again with a puzzled look on his face.

"Then, in another three months, I want you to do the same. In fact, I want you to repeat this every three months. Now, Mr. Hernández, you being an expert on plants and trees, tell me, what happens to those trees over time?"

Pops brushed his thin mustache with his fingers, thinking and thinking. "Well, Ms. Young," he answered, "the trees are not going to die, but I will tell you this: because you are transplanting the trees so much, you are not letting their roots grow deep. This will cause the trees to become weak to the point that it stunts their growth. They will remain small and fragile. And if they are fruit trees, I doubt they will even bear fruit."

Just as soon as he said this, he paused for a long moment. My father's facial expression changed. I could see that he understood the similarity between those trees and his four children.

"Oh, I see what you mean, Ms. Young," he confessed.

"I am so glad you do," Ms. Young said, and then went on to say goodbye as she made her way to the door. "I think my job is done here. Thank you for the lovely dinner, Mrs. Hernández and Mr. Hernández. You have some very intelligent kids."

After my teacher left the house, I could see Pops thinking over what had just occurred.

That year, when we drove through Southern California on our way back to California from Mexico, Pops did not veer right toward the Ontario-Chino area where we normally made our first stop. When we approached our second stop in Central California, Pops did not veer left toward the Salinas area, but kept driving north on Highway 99 to Stockton. Stockton would be our first and only stop. Although we still traveled to Mexico every year, instead of staying for three months, we only stayed for three weeks to celebrate Christmas and the Three Kings. Now, we only missed about one week of school each year. I could feel that our education was starting to gain traction. Soon my siblings and I were among the top performers in each of our classes.

But staying in one place had its price. Farm work was not readily available year round, and the long winter months were lean. I would remember Pops going out to work in the cold and foggy winter months to prune fruit trees and grapevines. It was also the rainy season, and when there was rain, there was no work. This type of on-again off-again work meant that Pops had barely enough money to pay the rent, gas, electricity, phone bills and buy the bare essentials, including groceries. The neighborhood market across the street from our house would give Pops credit in the winter. Once work picked up, Pops would promptly pay the grocery bill. Things started to get so lean that Pops ventured on to other types of jobs. Soon he learned how to drive trucks and got jobs that were not so seasonal.

And Pops knew how to make his own opportunities. He bought a used truck and started his own trucking business. Later he would buy more trucks and even hire a few drivers. Years later, when we were grown up, he was able to buy his first house, on nearly three acres of country property, where he and Mom retired.

CHAPTER 4

My Father's Recipe

The buzzer of my alarm went off in the bedroom of crew quarters. I had set the alarm for 7:30 in the morning. It was Friday, August 28, 2009, and we were going to space, I was convinced! After I showered, I headed toward the dining room, where most of my crewmates were already eating breakfast. I quickly put in my order for steak and eggs with hash browns and buttered wheat toast. Although the weather forecast called for a 60% go for launch, I could sense my crewmates' excitement. This was the third time we were officially getting ready for a launch.

The day began pretty much like the others. We had our meetings, lunch followed by more meetings, a very light dinner and our walk to the suit room to change. It was as if we were in a time machine; we repeated everything exactly as we had. We found ourselves once again in the suit room wearing our blue Spiderman LCVG suits, ready to put on the orange pumpkin LES suits. Soon, we once again rode down the elevator and made the short walk to the Astrovan. There was no shortage of Kennedy Space Center employees waiting outside and cheering us on as we made that short walk to the van and began our ride to launch pad 39A. This time, though, I was able to soak everything in and hear the cheers more clearly, look at the faces of the folks cheering, to wave at and acknowledge folks that I had worked with. I enjoyed the moment because I was not as nervous as I had been on the previous walks.

During the ride to the launch pad, CJ gave us a pep talk and said, "The weather is holding up, so stay sharp and focused."

The fact that I was able to see some stars in the partially cloudy night sky as I exited the Astrovan helped to convince me we would lift off this time. It would be our third attempt, and as the saying goes, the third time's a charm.

Just as we had done on Monday night, the whole crew strapped in without any problems. I crawled into the hatch, hopped on my seat and allowed the closeout crewmember to strap me in. Then, they put on my gloves and helmet, connected me to O2 and water for cooling and finally performed the communication or comm checks. We were now ready for the closeout crew to exit the vehicle, close the hatch, check for cabin leaks, disassemble the White Room and retract the access arm we had crawled through. As the crew descended and went to the fallback area, we started to follow our launch checklist. I told myself that if everything went well, we would be in space in a little less than three hours! As time progressed, so did the count-down clock.

"Everything looking nominal," I heard on the comm loops. This meant everything was operating as planned. We were closing in on the L minus 20-minute hold.

Soon, I observed the shuttle's onboard computers being configured for launch. The pilot initiated thermal conditioning of the fuel cells, and I called for our pilot to verify that the cabin vent valves were closed. About ten minutes or so into the hold, everything was going well, and we quickly found ourselves reaching the L minus 9-minute hold! During this final hold, I knew from previous launches that we had about 45 minutes of hold time left.

That's when I asked myself, *How in the heck did I get here?* I was ten years old the first time I thought about what I wanted to be when I grew up. It was December of 1972, and we lived on the corner of E and Vine Streets on the east side of Stockton. We were renting the same two-bedroom home Ms. Young had come to a few years back. In the living room, we had an old, console black and white television set topped off with a rabbit-ear antenna. I loved seeing the original *Star Trek* TV series. Between my stargazing at dawn, my astronomy book from Ms. Young *The Sun, the Moon and the Stars* and my love of *Star Trek,* it's no surprise space had captured my imagination. One very special event really solidified my dream of one day becoming a space explorer. It was none other than the real-life Apollo missions, the Apollo 17 moonwalks to be exact, that I saw on that old black and white television set. I was thrilled to follow the blastoff, splashdown and the astronauts walking on the moon.

I stood in awe to the side of the TV, adjusting the antenna, watching astronaut Eugene Cernan walk on the moon and talk to Mission Control Center in Houston. I also remember seeing and hearing the news-broadcaster Walter Cronkite narrate the moonwalk, giving lots of facts and figures regarding what would be the very last Apollo mission and moonwalk. (To date, we humans have not returned to the moon.) During the commercial breaks, I would go outside and see the almost-full moon in all its glory. Then I would run inside to see Astronaut Eugene Cernan walking on that same moon! *Wow,* I thought, *that is what I want to be! I want to be an astronaut!* That was how my dream of becoming an astronaut was born!

I am sure most every ten-year-old boy at that time in the United States—and in the world, for that matter—wanted to be an astronaut. However, I think the dream stayed with me because of what happened later that same evening. As we got ready for bed, Pops and I were walking toward the two bedrooms.

He was slightly in front of me when I called out to him and said, "Hey, Pops!"

"Yes, son?"

"I know what I want to be when I grow up."

"Yes, son, what is that?"

"I want to be an astronaut!"

Pops semi-stumbled and stopped dead in his tracks. He turned around, put his hand on his hip and said in a very challenging tone, "You want to be *what?*"

I was not fazed by his challenge because I was still excited from watching Eugene Cernan walk on the moon. So, I bravely answered, "I want to be an astronaut!"

Pops looked at me, raised his arm and pointed toward the kitchen. *"M'ijo,* let's go to the kitchen."

My eyes widened because I knew that we were told to go to the kitchen for three reasons: the first was to do our homework, the second was to eat and the third was that the kitchen was Pops' favorite place to apply "justice," which was his word for punishment!

I walked nervously, and Pops asked me to sit down. He sat down next to me and calmly asked me why I wanted to be an astronaut. I quickly blurted out everything I had learned about that evening's moonwalk.

Pops was impressed that I had the facts and figures down, such as the moon being almost a quarter million miles away, that it had no atmosphere and was covered with craters. More importantly, Pops saw the determination in his ten-year-old son's eyes to achieve something great in life.

What he said next really surprised me!

"I think you can do this, *m'ijo!*"

My eyes widened even more!

Then, he said, "If you really want to do this, you need to follow a very simple five-ingredient recipe I am going to give you."

"What's the recipe?" I asked with excitement! I was ready to absorb everything Pops was about to tell me! I asked again: "What's the recipe?"

"Okay," Pops said. "Pay attention. First, you have to decide what you want to be when you grow up."

"An astronaut," I blurted out and thought to myself that I had one out of the five already completed.

"Second," Pops said, "recognize how far you are from your goal."

I looked down at our linoleum kitchen floor and around at the grease-stained walls of our two-bedroom, dilapidated rental in the worst part of the east side of Stockton. "Well," I said, "we can't be any further than this, Pops!" At this point, I expected him to get mad, but surprisingly he did not!

Pops laughed a little and said, "I'm glad you recognize this, because the third ingredient is to draw yourself a roadmap from where you are to where you want to go. This roadmap will show you the way and keep you focused! Keep your eye on the prize, son!"

"What is the fourth ingredient?" I asked.

"Ah, you're doing this already, *m'ijo*: stay in school. There is no substitute for a good education! You need to go to college, because without that, there is no way you will reach your goal!" He paused, cleared his throat and said, "Fifth and finally, *m'ijo* . . . " He raised his arm and pointed out the kitchen window. "You know the effort you put in every time you pick strawberries, cherries, cucumbers, onions, green tomatoes, peaches and grapes?"

"Yes," I replied, a little bit puzzled, thinking of the weekends and summers of hard work in the fields.

"Well, you put that same effort here!" he said, pointing to my books on the kitchen table. "And when you get a job, you put that same effort into your job. Always, always give more than what is expected of you."

It was empowering to hear him speak like that! That evening, I went to sleep so happy. I thought, *Wow, Pops thinks I can become an astronaut! I am going to become one!* I quickly repeated Pops' five-ingredient recipe so as not to forget it:

1. Define what you want to do in life.
2. Recognize how far you are from your goal.
3. Draw yourself a roadmap.
4. Prepare yourself with a good education.
5. Develop a good work ethic and always give more than what is expected.

I have used the above recipe throughout my life and continue to use it, simply because it works!

CHAPTER 5

Third Time's a Charm: The Launch

As the communication traffic increased, I quickly realized that the nine-minute hold would soon be over. I could hear over the comm loop instructions for our pilot, Kevin Ford, to begin final preparations for the launch. Next, the NASA test director checked the weather forecasts for the Cape Canaveral area and verified that conditions met the agency's criteria for a safe launch and a safe landing in the event we had to abort the mission or return to the launch site.

Finally, our launch director, Pete Nickolenko, delivered one final message to our commander, CJ Sturckow: "The vehicle is clean and the team's a go. This time Mother Nature is cooperating. It looks like the third time really is a charm. We wish you and your team good luck and Godspeed."

"Thanks, Pete," CJ responded. "On behalf of the crew of Discovery, thanks to everyone who helped prepare for this mission. Let's go step up the science on the International Space Station."

Stepping Up Science was the official theme of our mission, quite appropriate since one of our payload or cargo items was a new treadmill we were delivering and installing on the space station.

Then, the countdown resumed. The access arm was now retracted at T minus 7 minutes and 30 seconds. The auxiliary power units were started at T minus 5 minutes, to assist in maneuvering the space shuttle, applying the brakes, steering, etc. . . . At T minus 3 minutes and 55 seconds, the wing flaps and rudder were positioned for launch; this is called the aerosurface profile test. The main engines were connected to

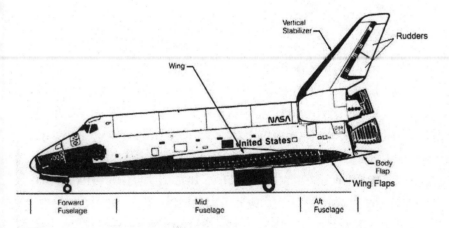

the shuttle by a kind of bearing called a gimbal that allowed each engine to be pivoted to help steer the shuttle (the way sails are positioned to help to steer a sailboat). These gimbals were tested and they were working perfectly.

At this point, I caught myself thinking that we were going to blast off this time! My excitement continued to build at T minus 2 minutes and 55 seconds, when CJ

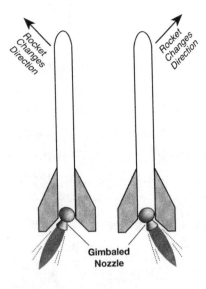

Gimbaled
Nozzle

announced, "There goes the beanie cap crew." The beanie cap was the gaseous oxygen vent arm that covered the top of the external tank. It prevented the super-cooled oxygen gas that evaporated from forming ice on the external tank that could damage the shuttle. It was now retracted.

About T minus 50 seconds, the shuttle transferred from ground to internal power, and at T minus 31 seconds, primary control of the countdown was transferred to the shuttle's onboard computers. At T minus 10 seconds, the hydrogen igniters were activated under each of the three engine bells. It was normal for some of the liquid hydrogen fuel to evaporate, but if there was too much, when the engine started the flammable gas could cause an explosion. At T minus six seconds, everything was functioning as it should, and the command was given to start the shuttle's three main engines.

At this point, I was happy to finally feel gentle vibrations when the three main engines came to life. It confirmed that everything was working. When we reached the T minus 0 mark the solid rocket boosters were ignited, then the noise thundered in my helmet and the shuttle shook like there was an earthquake. Just before liftoff, control was turned over from the Kennedy Space Center to the Johnson Space Center's Mission Control Center in Houston. In the instant before liftoff, I felt the Space Shuttle Discovery rock in a way that made me think it would either vibrate itself to pieces or fall flat on the ground. But shortly after this thought, I felt pressure on my back and heard through the comm loop, "We have liftoff!"

The liftoff was slow and gentle at first. Instead of enjoying the moment, as I was sure the three astronauts in the middeck were doing, the four of us in the flight deck were busy monitoring the instruments and following our ascent procedures checklist that we each had on our kneeboards (small clipboards that we keep on our knees throughout the ascent). As the flight engineer, my job was to monitor all the instruments for both pilots and call out predetermined milestones during the flight. If we were to have an anomaly, I would team up with either the pilot or the commander to work on the problem while the other pilot continued to perform the normal duties on our ascent checklist.

We had practiced launches hundreds of times on the motion-based simulators, so that our muscle memory took over for those eight-and-a-half critical minutes of powered flight. The pilots checked that shortly after liftoff the engines throttled up to 104.5%. They also checked that the shuttle had begun the maneuvers it would need to make. To the people watching the launch on land it looked like the space shuttle was rolling over, but these maneuvers were also putting us in the right heading (pilot-speak for direction) to be able to rendezvous with the International Space Station in orbit. The term for this maneuver is a combined roll, pitch and yaw.

Thirty seconds into the ascent, we verified that the three main engines throttled down to 72%, this point in our journey where we had to "step on the brakes" was called maximum dynamic pressure, or Max Q for short. Additionally, the Solid Rocket Boosters were designed to drop their thrust by about 30% fifty seconds into ascent. If you have ever seen a dog stick its head out the window of a moving car, you understand Max Q. The dog's ears flap around like crazy! While a car is designed to be able to travel at highway speeds, a dog is not. Every object has a maximum amount of pressure it can withstand.

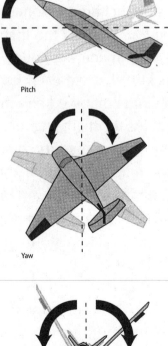

Pitch

Yaw

Roll

Failure to reduce the thrust would violate the structural limits of the space shuttle, causing severe to catastrophic damage! As the space shuttle climbed higher and higher in the atmosphere, the air pressure acting on the space shuttle decreased because the force of gravity also decreased. This allowed us to throttle the engine back to 104.5% once the shuttle's guidance verified that it was safe. This throttling down and back up, known as "thrust bucket," allowed the shuttle to go as fast as possible without risking structural damage.

At T plus 126 seconds, or 126 seconds after liftoff, it was time for the Solid Rocket Boosters (SRBs) to be disengaged from the External Tank/space shuttle. The bolts that connect the SRBs to the space shuttle carry an explosive charge; the charge was ignited and the SRBs, the largest motors in human history, were separated. Because they needed to get out of the way as soon as they were disengaged, each of the two SRBs were equipped with small rockets that propelled them away from the space shuttle. They were then parachuted down to about 200 miles off the coast of Florida, where they would be recovered by an awaiting NASA boat.

At almost six minutes into our ascent, the shuttle's direct communication link with the ground stations began to fade, at which point the shuttle rolled heads up to reroute its communication links to the Tracking and Data Relay Satellite system. It was at this point that we began to feel the G-forces acting against our bodies. When the G-force reached maximum 3 Gs or 96.5 ft/s², the equivalent to accelerating from zero to 65.8 mph (105.9 km/h) in just one second, the engines throttled back to maintain this maximum acceleration until we reached the 8-minute-and-30-second mark, known as the "main engine cutoff" or MECO for short.

Toward the end of the 8 minutes and 30 seconds of powered flight, I found it very hard to raise my arms because the G-forces were at their maximum. As soon as the external tank was released by firing the pyrotechnic fasteners and we were no longer accelerating, the feeling of a big, 400-pound gorilla on my chest suddenly disappeared.

We were now coasting at our final speed of 17,500 mph and would do so for another thirty minutes as we reached the furthest point of our slightly elliptical orbit known as apogee. It was at that point that our commander and pilot fired the two Orbiter Maneuvering System engines. They put us on the path to the desired orbit, approximately 240 miles above ground. That occurred while the external tank fell back into the atmosphere and disintegrated into thousands of small pieces somewhere between the Indian and Pacific oceans. The shuttle was now on the same plane and height as the International Space Station, although slightly behind it, going around the earth once every ninety minutes.

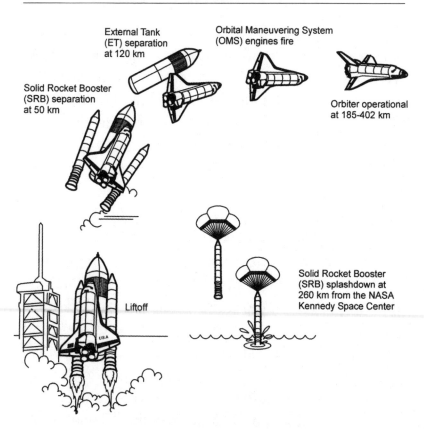

External Tank
(ET) separation
at 120 km

Orbital Maneuvering System
(OMS) engines fire

Solid Rocket Booster
(SRB) separation
at 50 km

Orbiter operational
at 185-402 km

Liftoff

Solid Rocket Booster
(SRB) splashdown at
260 km from the NASA
Kennedy Space Center

Flight Day 1

When we entered orbit, I considered myself an official astronaut. I was finally in space experiencing microgravity! Our three crewmates in the middeck had unbuckled from their seats and were floating around, while we four in the flight deck were still firm in our seats, held by our five-point harnesses. The crew in the flight deck still had approximately an hour more work to perform, including reconfiguring the vehicle from launch mode to orbit operations mode, which meant purging fuel lines and activating life support systems, among other items on our checklist. As we did this, I could hear and sometimes see our middeck crewmates floating from the middeck into our flight deck as they performed their individual and group tasks. In essence, every five-minute segment for each of the seven crewmembers for the next fourteen days was accounted for in a timeline of tasks.

Finally, the time came when those of us on the flight deck were able to remove our seatbelts! As I unbuckled, I slowly began to elevate off my chair and pushed off to propel myself from the flight deck into the entrance of the middeck. I saw that the middeck crew was already working on activating the kitchen galley, the bathroom and getting ready to open the payload bay doors. It was necessary to open them soon after we reached space because the radiators were on the inside wall of these doors and would run the coolant loops that would keep our electronics and cabin at an appropriate temperature. Our commander had control of our cabin temperature and, luckily for us, he kept it at a very comfortable level.

The next thing they worked on was deploying the Ku-Band Antenna, followed by the installation of the stationary bicycle. Each crewmember had to exercise on this bike about forty minutes a day to maintain the strength of our leg muscles. That was because in the microgravity of space, we were constantly floating and did not utilize our legs enough. Failing to exercise would weaken the muscles, causing them to atrophy and make it extremely difficult to walk once we returned from space.

My first job after leaving my seat was to install the portable on-board computers. These computers were to be networked together by cables. They would inter-face with the shuttle's sensors. They would allow us to be aware of our surroundings during our rendezvous with the International Space Station (ISS). This aware-ness was needed because we would dock with the ISS while both vehicles traveled at about 17,500 mph. per hour. My schedule allowed a certain amount of time for me to work on this task. When I finished some ten minutes early, I went to see if anyone needed help with the task on his or her timeline.

So much of the day was taken up by the launch that it was already time to eat dinner and turn in for the night. During training, we had tasted more than 100 samples of main entrees, sides, desserts and drinks. These included chicken with rice, mac and cheese, hamburger meat, shrimp cocktail, chocolate cake, cookies, coffee, tea and other items. Most of the food was dehydrated and came in packets. Other foods came in the form of military rations. Once we picked out the foods we liked, the NASA nutritionist created a balanced diet for our fourteen days in space.

Our onboard food was marked with different col-ored stickers for each crewmember. My color code was green. I picked up my food selections and added hot or cold water to each container, heated the items that needed heating, cut open the containers with a small pair of scissors and began to eat my first meal, alongside my crewmates, in space.

Eating in space was a bit tricky because everything floats! Although the food bags had a bit of Velcro that could be attached to Velcro on the galley table, it was sometimes easier to eat your items one after the other. If you did not, you ran the risk of your food floating away. Something as simple as scooping peas out of a bag and stopping your spoon too far from your mouth could cause the peas to shoot out from the spoon and spread apart, much like the pellets coming out of a shotgun!

Eating our meals in microgravity was sloppy at first, but as the days went on, we became experts. Another odd thing was that bread was not often available in space. We astronauts preferred, of all things, tortillas. And because we had two Mexican-American astronauts, which was a first, many mornings Danny Olivas and I made scrambled eggs and cheese breakfast burritos for the crew. I think Danny and I can claim having operated the first taco truck in space!

Sleeping in space was also a very interesting experience. We ran our days and nights to coincide with Houston time. Most of us would change into a T-shirt and shorts; retrieve our sleeping bags and claim a bit of real estate in the middeck, which would from then on be our night quarters. We would tie down the four corners of our sleeping bags to the wall or the floor so

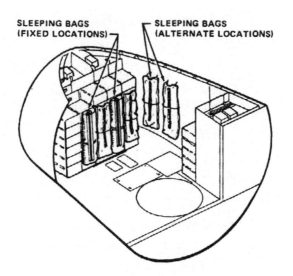

SLEEPING BAGS (FIXED LOCATIONS) — SLEEPING BAGS (ALTERNATE LOCATIONS)

that they would not float away. Our pilots would sleep in the flight deck.

As I mentioned earlier, we were traveling at 17,500 mph, miles per hour, and we were orbiting the Earth every ninety minutes. That meant we had approximately 45 minutes of daylight and 45 minutes of darkness on a continuous basis. To get a good night's sleep, we had to turn off the lights and draw the shades on the windows so that the sun's light would not interfere with our sleep. This was especially true in the flight deck, where the windows are larger and more numerous.

Once we set up our sleeping bags, we would gently float into them and zip ourselves up; the bags had slits on the sides so our arms could come out to zip ourselves up. It was strange that a pillow was useless in space, because in microgravity your head floats; it does not need to be propped up. And since we were literally floating in our sleeping bags, we had the perfect mattresses.

When I floated into my sleeping bag, I noticed zero pressure points on my body. It took a couple of nights for me to get used to not having a pillow, but I still got the best sleep I ever had during that fourteen-day mission! As I was dozing off, I could hear the background noises similar to those in a science lab, where you hear the noise of pumps, fans and the A/C.

After the lights were turned off and I was lying inside my sleeping bag, I put in my earplugs to silence most of the noise, but I could still hear the alarm if it went off. I pinched myself and asked, *Am I really getting ready to spend my first evening sleeping in space?* Once again, I caught myself thinking about the journey that had brought me to this point. I thought about Pops' recipe and about how lucky I was to have him, my mother and my older siblings. They had guided me through the most critical times of my life: my pre-teen and teenage years.

CHAPTER 6

Staying Focused

One of the points in my life where things might have gone wrong was when I started to attend Fremont Junior High School for grades 7, 8 and 9. My world opened up as I was exposed to new things, bigger kids and bigger problems. I was in the seventh grade and eighth and ninth graders usually picked on kids in lower grades. Luckily, many of the students knew my older siblings, Gil and Lety, who were respectively in the eighth and ninth grades and this played to my advantage. It was also hard to develop a relationship with my teachers because we had seven different subjects and each had a different teacher. Unlike in elementary school, the students did not just come from our immediate neighborhood but from all over the area. I was surprised at their rowdy behavior and even more so at some of the teachers' inability to control the rowdiest of students.

We were also exposed to the drug culture. Getting drugs was as easy as going to the restroom. You could buy them from any of the handful of students who were selling them.

Starting junior high school also felt overwhelming because my oldest brother, Sal, had been sent to Mexico so that he could attend high school there. My parents planned on the whole family moving back to Michoacán eventually, and so they sent Sal to get a head start. Mom and Pops wanted him to be well adjusted so that he would not struggle in college there. It seemed reasonable at the time; little did we know that our home would eventually end up being in California. Perhaps what helped shape this was my sister Lety finishing junior high. She was not sent to Mexico to be on her own because she was a girl. Hispanic parents are very protective of the girls in the family, and in this case, it worked to Lety's advantage. Once she started high school and my parents saw that she was doing well, they decided that Gil and me could attend high school in California.

Sal visited and worked with us each summer in California. I could see that he yearned to stay with us. Eventually, Sal finished high school in La Piedad and moved to Morelia, the capital city of the state of Michoacán, to attend college. I remember all of us being so proud of him, especially because he was studying electrical engineering. Sal eventually graduated and came back to California to work as an engineer. However, I think he still holds a bit of resentment toward the family for sending him to Mexico. I cannot say I blame him, but I also think my parents thought they were doing what was best for him.

I started Fremont Junior High School with three of my best friends from our neighborhood. Two of them, Alberto and Carlos, were brothers one year apart but in the same grade, and the third, Sergio, lived across the street from me. When I first met Alberto and Carlos, they were relatively new to the States and knew very little English. Like me, they were migrant farmworkers who also settled in Stockton and still did farm work on weekends and seven days a week during summer vacations. Alberto and Carlos' father was a hard worker but unfortunately drank a lot of alcohol. Sergio, on the other hand, was born in the United States but had a father who had many vices, including gambling, alcohol and women; he was hardly ever at home. His family was large and always on public assistance. In the seventh grade, we had classes together. Alberto and Sergio were good students, but Carlos and I were always at the top of the class and we openly competed against each other. I have to confess that Carlos beat my test scores more often than I beat his.

During the summer between the seventh and eighth grades, we had little contact with each other because our families worked for different growers. After working in the fields, my father and mother kept a tight rein on us and did not allow us to venture beyond our block. Though I saw and talked to Sergio every once in a while, I was too tired after work to even think about accepting his invitations to hang out with him, Alberto and Carlos. In retrospect, I think my parents sensed the danger of me developing too close of a relationship with them. Somehow, they knew that these were at-risk kids and wanted to make sure that I only hung out with them on our street where they could keep an eye on us.

When we started the eighth grade, I sensed an immediate change in my three neighborhood friends. All of sudden, Carlos was not interested in competing against me for the best grade in the class, and Alberto and Sergio went from being good students to performing poorly. It was as if they did not care and were just going through the motions at school. I also noticed that their wardrobe was changing. Before, they had worn regular clothes, but they had started to wear the traditional clothing of *cholos*: well-ironed khaki pants, a white T-shirt with a plaid Pendleton, long-sleeved shirt and shiny, black Stacy Adams shoes. They started to hang out with new friends I did not recognize from our neighborhood, who dressed just like them. It was in the ninth grade that I realized that my friends were not interested in going to high school; they started cutting classes, getting into fights and experimenting with drugs.

It was then that I stopped hanging out with my best friends. They started taunting me, calling me "school boy" for refusing to cut class with them.

Maybe it was the fear of disappointing my parents, or that I knew I wanted to go to college and become an astronaut that kept me on the straight and narrow. Regardless, I plowed ahead with my studies at Fremont and looked forward to starting high school.

I remember being excited about starting high school and being happy that I would not be in the lowest grade. That year they converted our junior high schools into middle schools, which meant that two grade levels would be starting at Franklin High School. I was in the incoming group of tenth-graders. The fact that my brother Gil was now a junior and my sister Lety a senior there made me feel at ease because I would be known as their younger brother.

Franklin High School was the first school that was too far from home to walk to. It was a good five miles away. I had it easy because by that time Lety and Gil were driving. My father had made enough money driving trucks to buy them a used but sporty-looking, green 1969 Oldsmobile Cutlass Supreme. I called it the Green Hornet. It was in this car that all four of us learned to drive.

When Lety graduated from Franklin High School, she went off to study at Humphries College in Stockton and needed the Green Hornet to get to school. This meant Gil and I needed another car. It was that summer when Gil and Pops bought a white 1972 Mercury Montego. This would be the car Gil and I would take to school. Gil was mechanically talented and fitted the car with new rims and lights and lowered it to blend in somewhat with the lowriders in our neighborhood. I say "somewhat" because we never considered ourselves *cholos*, but we did want to blend in and not call attention to ourselves.

High school was where I came out of my shell and started to develop friendships with students who were not from my neighborhood and who came from different backgrounds. During my junior year, I remember still being embarrassed by where we lived, by our financial situation and the fact that we still did farm work. I was so embarrassed that I even avoided inviting friends home. Part of getting out of my shell had to do with being involved in high school soccer and student government. I remember the fall of my junior year sitting in a meeting discussing the homecoming float that our class was supposed to build. The only problem was that no one had access to a truck and flatbed trailer. No one, that is, except me, because by this time Pops had just bought a used one for his work as a self-employed truck driver. But if I volunteered Pops' vehicles, I knew he would want us to build the float at our house, where he kept them.

I finally offered to ask Pops if we could use his one and driving expertise for the parade. Pops agreed, but said the float had to be worked on in front of our house, just as I suspected. We had about a week's worth of work to do in turning the flatbed into a viable float. Every day that week, the junior class would stop over at our house and work on the float. My family even got into the act, with Mom bringing out food, typically burritos and *agua de Jamaica,* a hibiscus drink. My father would bring out the boom box and let us set it to a station we liked. Even my brother and sister came out to help.

A few days into building the float, I marveled at how each day the number of students coming out to help us had increased; they seemed to enjoy the burritos that I had been embarrassed to bring to school for lunch. They also enjoyed the *agua fresca* and the company of my parents and siblings. One of my friends who had just gotten a new car from his mom even came up to me and told me how lucky I was.

"Lucky?" I said. "Why?"

"Because, even though my neighborhood might be richer and I have a brand-new Camaro . . . every day after school I go home to an empty house. My parents are divorced . . . I live with my mom. She's a nurse and always has to work."

Wow! That's when I really understood the value of a close-knit family. To think, I had been too busy being embarrassed about our economic situation to appreciate what so many of my classmates did not have: a stable and loving home environment and pride in their family's cultural heritage. I was also lucky to have the opportunity to take the best parts of the two cultures I lived in to define myself as an individual. No longer would I live in two distinct worlds, but rather I would serve as a bridge that merged both of my worlds.

High school was going great for me. I was thriving academically. I was involved in sports and was part of student leadership. I had many teachers who inspired me to learn and to keep learning. There was Mrs. Sylvia Bello, who taught us Spanish and biology. Mrs. Bello was as strict as they came but she was also fair. She demanded a lot but also gave a lot of herself. She would sell burritos in her class to help us raise funds for excursions to Mexico when she taught Spanish, and did the same for trips to Baja California when she taught biology. I joined her two Spanish class trips to Guadalajara. To keep costs down our class traveled by bus and stayed at a group home for the blind. I also traveled with her to Baja California, where we camped during spring break and studied plant taxonomy and marine biology.

My biggest influence in math was Mr. David Ellis, who taught us in middle and high school. In middle school, there were six of us who took all the math classes offered but still had a year left before graduation. Mr. Ellis took it upon himself to create a calculus course for the six of us. In high school, Mr. Ellis, Mrs. Bello and a few other teachers followed us. These pre-college teachers had a big impact on my life, including Mr. Alameda, who taught me the fundamentals of chemistry and physics. Then there was Mr. Zendejas, who took an interest in helping me get into college and helped me fill out my college applications and write the essay about who I was and why I wanted to go to college. To this day, I stay in touch with all of these teachers who have since retired.

In high school, I played on the varsity soccer team as a center forward and was the lead scorer during my senior year. But I knew that I was not good enough to get an athletic scholarship for college, much less play professionally. Knowing this took some of the pressure off and allowed me to thrive and really enjoy playing on the team. I also got involved in student leadership at the beginning of my junior year and quickly found myself being encouraged to run for student body president. The only problem was that there were two other candidates running as well. And both of them were very popular! I knew I would face an uphill battle if I were to jump into the race. Nevertheless, with encouragement from both students and teachers, I decided I had nothing to lose. I announced that I would run. The campaign amounted to posters, flyers and an assembly where we each gave a speech as to why we should be elected. I also conducted what I called a grassroots effort to convince the students to vote for me. The popular kids hardly campaigned, but I worked hard and focused on students in the English as a Second Language program, or what I referred to as the "forgotten population." They had as much right to vote as any other student. I made a concerted effort to go to their classes and speak in Spanish. I am convinced these students' votes led me to victory. The next school year I would be the student body president!

When my brother Gil graduated from high school, he decided to attend Spartan School of Aeronautics in Tulsa, Oklahoma, which meant his Mercury Montego would travel with him. He would stay there two years and get his airframe and power plant technician certification. The summer before Gil graduated, we started to get jobs that did not involve farm work. During the school year, Gil and I worked at a restaurant as dishwashers, kitchen prep, busboys and even as waiters. In the summers, we kept those jobs, but also participated in federally funded summer youth employment programs working as custodians in none other than my own Fremont Junior High that was now called Fremont Middle School. I remember mopping, waxing and buffing the classroom floors. I also painted the hallway walls my friends used to spray paint with graffiti.

As Gil got ready to leave for Oklahoma, I realized I would need my own car and asked Pops if he would help me find one. Pops obliged, and I quickly found myself to be the proud owner of a 1964 Chevrolet Impala. Though the car was older than Lety's Green Hornet or Gil's Mercury Montego, the Impala was a Super Sport model that had bucket seats and a 327 engine block. It was jet black and had pin-striped roses painted on the sides. In our neighborhood, this car definitely fit in. I joked that it was the "president's car" and nicknamed her "Rosie."

Flight Day 2

Surprisingly, 6:00 am arrived quickly, and we were awakened by the music the crew had selected. Since our mission was for fourteen days, our crewmembers got to select two songs each. Commander CJ Sturckow had selected the song that played that first morning. It was customary that whoever's song played that morning would greet Mission Control Houston over comm and say a word or two related to the song they had selected. My songs were played on the mornings of Days 4 and 9. The first song I had selected was Gloria Estefan's "Mi Tierra," which I chose because Tierra means Earth. Later that evening, I received an email that Gloria Estefan sent to NASA's public affairs office to thank me for playing her song in space. She wrote that her mother said she knew Gloria had made it big when she heard her song was being played in space. The second song was one from my father's era, José Alfredo Jiménez's "El Hijo del Pueblo," meaning "son of the people." This one reminisced about being born poor, of having common roots and a big heart. I dedicated this one to Pops. My mother later told me that tears rolled down Pops' cheeks as he heard the song and dedication live on the NASA channel.

After getting up that morning, we floated out of our sleeping bags and stowed them, cleaned up and ate breakfast. Next, we started our individual tasks. Flight Day 2 included several of us performing a survey of

Discovery's thermal protection system. When we would re-enter the Earth's atmosphere, we would do so at a temperature of 3,000 degrees Fahrenheit. We used the shuttle's robotic arm coupled to the orbiter boom sensor system to make sure the thermal protection system was intact. Ever since the Space Shuttle Columbia had disintegrated upon re-entering Earth's gravity because of damage to the material that covered the wing to protect it from the searing heat, this had become a necessary inspection.

While we worked on this task, my other colleagues checked out the suits for walking in space. They also installed the centerline camera that would allow the commander and pilot to see the International Space Station and maneuver into the dock, and extended the orbiter docking system ring that would connect the shuttle to the International Space Station like a plug in an outlet. Later that day, I turned on the portable computers and checked the software tools that would be used for our rendezvous with the International Space Station. These tools would give us the visual queues we needed for speed and alignment to successfully dock to the space station.

Aside from doing our major tasks, we also had a host of smaller ones. While we did these non-critical tasks, we grew to appreciate the advantages of gravity as we experience it back on Earth. For example, one of my first non-critical duties on Day 2 was to replace the cabin air filter, a task we practiced a few times during our training runs. The task essentially involved grabbing a screwdriver, unscrewing the four screws to remove the panel, replacing the filter and reinstalling the panel with the screws. Simple, right?

Well, when I positioned myself to unscrew the first screw, I was floating and hovering above the panel. As I went to loosen the screw in a counter clockwise direction, I quickly found my whole body torqueing the opposite way! *Makes sense,* I thought, *since this was what Newton's third law stated: For every action, there is an equal and opposite reaction.* Upon making sure no one was watching me embarrass myself, I noticed that on the floor of the deck there were foot straps. I gently slipped my feet into the two loops, and problem solved! I was firmly anchored and now able to go about my business of unscrewing the four screws that held the panel in place. Then, I quickly found out that I needed duct tape to hold the screws I had removed or they would float away. We had not been taught those little things during our ground training sessions. I think they left them out on purpose, just so that the veteran astronauts could amuse themselves seeing us first-time flyers struggle with those issues.

Flight Day 2 was our first complete day in space and everything went as planned. There were no anomalies to report, and once again, after a hearty meal of chicken with rice, peas, punch and strawberries and cream, it was time for bed. The drill was the same as the night before, but the setup went quicker because everyone already had his or her territory staked out. Slipping into the sleeping bag was somewhat easier; I was getting used to microgravity. *Tomorrow,* I thought, *we would physically dock to the International Space Station and meet our colleagues in space.* As I started to fall asleep, I thought about that last year in high school.

CHAPTER 7

Following the Roadmap

My senior year in high school was a great year. I was driving Rosie to school by myself every day, was on the varsity soccer team and was the student body president of Franklin High School. I also knew I was college-bound, although I did not know which university I would attend nor how I was going to pay for it. I had heard rumors about how expensive it was to attend college and how some of my friends' parents had a college fund for them. "College fund?" I asked. We barely had enough to pay the monthly bills, let alone save for college!

The one thing I knew I had to do that fall was to take the SAT test and apply to universities. I had a part-time job as a busboy at a seafood restaurant where I worked the dinner shift. This allowed me to do farm work occasionally on weekends. It was on one of those weekends that I was hoeing baby sugar beet plants when I heard the news on my transistor radio that NASA had just selected the first Hispanic-American astronaut. It brought back the dream that I had relegated to the back of my mind. The "first

Hispanic-American astronaut" was what I kept thinking. Truth be told, I was a little disappointed that I would not be the first. However, I was glad that someone was paving the way for other aspiring Hispanic Americans like me. All I could think of that day was finishing the work on that sugar beet field so that I could go home and follow up on this exciting news. Once the workday finally came to an end, I went home, showered and began investigating who Franklin Chang-Díaz was. It took me several days, but I found out that Dr. Chang-Díaz came from humble beginnings, like me. When I heard him speak in a radio interview, he spoke with an accent, like me. And when I saw him on TV, he had brown skin, like me. Most importantly, Franklin Chang-Díaz had a college education, including a Ph.D., *Unlike me,* I thought, *but not for long.*

The news about Dr. Franklin Chang-Díaz made me revisit Pops' recipe to ensure I was following it to a T. Pops had said to:

1. Define what you want to do in life.
2. Recognize how far you are from your goal.
3. Draw yourself a roadmap.
4. Prepare yourself with a good education.
5. Develop a good work ethic and always give more than what is expected.

When I looked at Pops' recipe, I convinced myself that I was still on the right path. Although I needed to work harder at Step 3, it was only a matter of time before I would complete Step 4. Still, I felt a sense of urgency, I wanted to start college right away and not waste any time. Dr. Chang-Díaz's selection by NASA demonstrated the importance for kids of role models that look like them. Although I'm sure I still would have pursued my dream of becoming an astronaut, Dr. Chang-Díaz's selection made me realize becoming an astronaut was indeed an achievable goal. It gave me a sense of empowerment, and this sense was very similar to how I felt when Pops had given me the recipe above.

Flight Day 3

Our 6:00 am wake-up call came to the tune of "Made to Love" by Toby Mac, which was selected by Astronaut Nicole Stott's ten-year-old son, Roman. She also sent him a "ginormous" thanks and big space hugs, which made me miss my own kids. Today was going to be a special day, as the timeline called for us to ren-dezvous and physically dock to the International Space Station. But before this could happen, CJ, our com-mander, would perform what's called a "rendezvous pitch maneuver," which is a fancy term for pitching the nose down and continuing to do so until you perform a 360-degree turn. Once the bottom portion of the shuttle faced the International Space Station, two astronauts on the station—Russian cosmonaut and Expedition 20 Commander Gennady Padalka and Expedition 20 flight engineer Michael Barrett—would take pictures of the shuttle's thermal protection, located on the underbelly region and the wing leading edges of the shuttle.

In addition to the boom inspection we had conducted the previous flight day, those high-resolution photographs were part of the new protocol. This was a result of the Columbia Space Shuttle accident. The ground team before our re-entry wanted to ensure that no damage had occurred during our ascent. Columbia had sustained damage to its thermal protection, so much so that the heat generated during re-entry penetrated the inside portion of the wing, which caused the wing to disintegrate from the inside and the shuttle to crash. All seven crewmembers had died. This accident was a solemn reminder that space exploration was far from a routine activity. The high-resolution photographs would also show any damage from a micrometeorite or piece of orbital debris hitting the shuttle, because just as hail can damage a car, flying space rocks can damage a space shuttle.

With the success of this maneuver, we were given the "go for docking," which meant that we would begin utilizing the propulsion jets to maneuver us closer and closer to the space station until Discovery would physically dock and latch onto the pressurized mating adapter on the front of the International Space Station Harmony module.

This operation may sound easy, but it takes the concentration of the whole shuttle crew to ensure both pilots receive the necessary information to come in on target, in plane and at just the right approach speed. Remember, this is done at 17,500 mph, and coming in too fast might cause us to bounce away from the docking mechanism. Coming in off-plane might cause us to damage the latching mechanism and even get it stuck. Needless to say, coming in off-target would cause structural damage to both the shuttle and the space station. As the flight engineer, I was in front of the computers verbalizing targeting, distance and approach speed to both pilots, while others were operating a hand-held laser, taking still photographs and video or in direct contact with Mission Control in Houston.

As we prepped for activating the thruster jets, everything seemed nominal, normal. We began using a combination of primary thrusters to give us large-scale corrections while the smaller Vernier jets provided the fine adjustments. Halfway through our docking maneuvers, we found that the Vernier jets began to fail; we were left with only our primary jets to perform the docking. No worries, though, as this was a scenario we had practiced during our training in the simulators. It only made the job harder for our pilots because they had no way to make the small, fine adjustments they were used to making. As we approached the target, we could see we were moving coarsely from side to side, and CJ would have to time it such that when I called our distance of 3 ft., his side-to-side movement would end up center on target at 0 ft. Like the good Marine pilot that he is, he nailed it, and we successfully docked to the station.

The crew celebrated by congratulating each other with handshakes and high fives.

Once docked, the pressurization of the docking compartment allowed us to open our respective hatches. This created a tunnel that allowed us to go back and forth between the shuttle and the space station. When we entered the space station, its commander rang what looked like a Navy bell to announce our arrival. The six station crewmembers seemed genuinely happy to see the seven Discovery crewmembers. Later, I would find out that all of them had been up in space for months and were tired of eating dehydrated food. A new crew meant fresh fruits and vegetables!

After the safety briefing and a tour of the space station, which included the Russian, US, European and Japanese experiment modules, our Discovery crewmember, Nicole Stott, switched Soyuz seat liners with Expedition 20 flight engineer Tim Kopra. Soyuz is the Russian word for "union" which makes sense since it is a shuttle that docks to the ISS. Depending on ISS crew size, one or two of them are docked at the ISS at all times in case an escape is necessary. The seat liner officially made Nicole Stott an Expedition 20 member and Tim Kopra a member of the Discovery crew. This crew exchange was the first of three major goals of our mission; Tim Kopra would return with us while Nicole stayed behind to complete her three-month mission on the space station. The second goal was to unload and install more than seven tons of equipment inside the Italian-built Multi-Purpose Logistics

Module, our cargo we affectionately called Leonardo that was located in our payload bay.

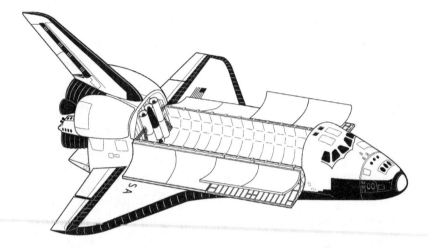

The third major goal was to conduct three space-walks. There was lots of work to do on these spacewalks; astronauts had to replace a spent ammonia tank crucial to the External Thermal Control System that circulates liquid ammonia coolant (when the space station is in the sun, it can reach a temperature of up to 250 degrees). They had to attach avionics cables that would allow for life-support, thermal control and communication systems to be ready to go before installation of the node Tranquility (the different rooms or chambers of the space station are called nodes). Finally, they had to replace a Gyro assembly (a tool for navigation) and install two GPS antennas among other smaller tasks.

It was amazing how the perception of small, con-fined quarters changed once you started operating in microgravity. I remember doing our training in a 1-G environment in actual-size replicas of the middeck and flight deck and wondering how all seven crewmem bers would be able to fit, let alone work. However, once in space, I found that because we were floating and there was no floor, our working space more than doubled. During the first two days on the space shuttle, I did not feel cramped. And once we were docked to the space station, it seemed like a palace. A day or two would go by without me seeing one of my colleagues, as we were all busy doing our jobs.

I also have to say that the space station was a thing of beauty. To think that seventeen countries contributed to the construction of this amazing orbiting laboratory whose outer structure is the size of a football field!

When we got ready for bed at the end of Flight Day 3, I noticed that a couple of our crewmembers chose to sleep in the space station. As the flight engineer, I

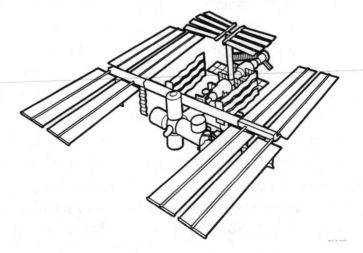

chose to stay on the shuttle, in the event any alarms went off during the night. Sleeping in a micro-G environment was getting easier because I was getting used to sleeping without a pillow.

Flight Day 4

Flight Day 4 was the first full day both crews would work together. The six-person-crew on the space station had their own timelines, but they were closely coordinated with our timelines and objectives. The command of the space station alternated between the two biggest contributors to the station, which were the United States and Russia, with each country getting command duties every six months. In our case, the commander was the Russian Gennady Padalka, which pleased me because I got the opportunity to practice my Russian-language skills. He seemed appreciative of the fact that in non-critical situations I would always try to talk to him in Russian. I say non-critical because the official language in the space station is English.

Day 4 was another jam-packed day, as we would unberth the Multi-Purpose Logistics Module (MPLM) from Discovery's payload bay and install it on the Earth-facing port of the space station node. Our pilot, Kevin Ford, would operate the station's robotic arm, grapple the MPLM, unberth it from the cargo bay, move it and install it on the node.

I would get the honor of doing exactly the opposite toward the end of our mission; we would bring back

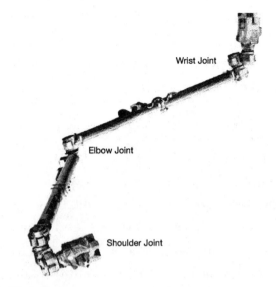

Wrist Joint

Elbow Joint

Shoulder Joint

The ISS robotic arm.

home the MPLM half-full with trash, dirty clothing, material from experiments that had been completed and anything else the space station did not need.

As Kevin and other colleagues worked on docking the MPLM, I worked with our first two spacewalkers, Danny Olivas and Nicole Stott, as well as with our new Discovery crewmate, Tim Kopra, to get the space suits ready for the next day's spacewalks, also known as "extravehicular activities." Tim and I took tool inventory and prepped the ones they were going to use while Danny and Nicole reviewed their space-walk procedures, and went over last-minute details with Mission Control. While we were preparing for the spacewalk, Kevin and his team had successfully docked the MPLM, pressurized it and opened its hatch, thus giving us access to the more than seven tons of equipment and supplies inside.

We ate dinner at the end of the workday and then assisted Danny and Nicole in preparing their camp out evening in the Quest Airlock. The airlock is the chamber where astronauts can exit the space station into space. There is no "air" in space. The molecules of nitrogen and oxygen we need to breathe are found on the surface of the earth because of gravity. Breathing in space is like breathing underwater; it requires special equipment.

The airlock is equipped with tanks of nitrogen and oxygen so that when they return from their spacewalk they can close the hatch and repressurize the airlock, open the inner hatch, remove their helmets and breathe. Astronauts sleep in the airlock before performing a spacewalk to reduce the risk of decompression sickness. It has lower air pressure (10.2 psi) compared to the normal station pressure of 14.7 psi. This lower pressure helps to flush nitrogen, preventing the formation of gas bubbles in the body that could lead to decompression sickness; this sickness has also been known to affect scuba divers and is sometimes called "the bends."

Flight Day 5

The morning of Day 5 began by getting both Danny and Nicole ready for their spacewalk. Tim Kopra and I helped them get into their white space suits, similar to but not the same as I had first seen on TV in 1972 during the Apollo 17 moonwalk. This process took a few hours because we had to perform many checks in coordination with Mission Control. We had to see of there were leaks in the suit and check the life support and communications systems, as well as the camera and lamp. Remember: we were orbiting Earth at a height of about 250 miles, going around the world once every ninety minutes. That meant that my colleagues would be working outside in sequences of 45 minutes of daylight followed by 45 minutes of darkness. Time was very valuable because of limited consumables, such as battery power and air supply. It was important for them to keep working through the dark phase of each orbit, but they could only do so if they had functioning lights on their helmets.

Danny and Nicole had three main tasks during their more than six hours outside the space station. First, they removed and stowed an empty ammonia tank assembly. Then they removed the European technology exposure facility, which was a platform for nine experiments. Lastly, they removed the rack for the space station's Experiment 6, which was a box used for testing the effects of exposure of various materials to the space environment.

While Danny and Nicole were out conducting their spacewalk, Pat Forrester gave them assistance with their procedures. I was helping Christer Fuglesang and space station member Frank De Winne with the transfer of experiments from the shuttle to the space station. We moved the new crew quarters, an exercise treadmill and the rack for the air revitalization system. Six hours later the spacewalk had been successful. After they entered the airlock and sealed the outside hatch, we pressurized the airlock and then opened our access hatch to the airlock and pulled them into the space station, where we helped them get out of their suits. After being outside for more than six hours, they were tired and hungry.

That evening during dinner, Danny and Nicole talked about their walk and the lessons learned that could be applied to the next two upcoming spacewalks. It was finally time to go to bed. It had been an especially busy day. As usual, I floated into my sleeping bag. Instead of putting on my headphones, I decided to take a moment to appreciate the fact that we were almost halfway through our mission. Up to that point, I had thought about my life as a kid, but not about my struggles in college and how I navigated my career to get to where I was.

It seemed that my senior year in high school was ending about as quickly as it had started. I had applied and was accepted to several colleges, including the University of the Pacific, which I chose to attend because I could save money by living at home. Every other school I was accepted to was far away and required me to live on campus. At the University of the

Pacific, I was accepted into the Community Involve-
ment Program that, when combined with my other
grants and work-study, covered up to 90% of my
tuition. *It was a good deal,* I thought, but the University
of the Pacific was a private school, which meant I still
had to come up with almost three thousand dollars for
tuition each year.

I was lucky to have a high school counselor, Mr.
Vance Paulsen, who not only helped me with college
applications but also helped me get a summer job at
a cannery for ketchup, tomatoes, spaghetti sauce and
fruit cocktail. The job paid a lot more than any other
summer job I ever had and allowed me to raise most
of the money for my tuition. The other jobs during the
school year provided the rest of the funds I needed to
pay for my books and gas. The cannery job had one
little inconvenience: it overlapped a few weeks with
the start of college. So, for about three weeks I worked
from 10 at night to six in the morning, went home to
shower and then drove to the university for class from
8 am to 3 pm. I would then do homework for three
hours, sleep another three and then go to work again
at 10 pm. It was tough, but I couldn't just quit the job
when school started because then I would not be
rehired the following summer. To make matters worse,
the following summer the overlap period increased by
two weeks due to my seniority.

At the University of the Pacific, where most students came from affluent families, I stood out like a

sore thumb. I was a sight to see, driving to campus in my lowrider, jet black 1964 Chevy Impala Super Sport. I was at times mistaken for a local high school dropouts coming to campus to get tutoring for the General Equivalency Diploma (GED), even by the university president himself!

My major was electrical engineering, which meant I took Calculus 1, Chemistry, Fortran Programming and Intro to Engineering that very first semester. Working nights and having this courseload was tough because, even though I was an A-student at Franklin High School, the students at Pacific seemed so much more prepared. After taking my first set of midterms and seeing the not-so-good results, I started to doubt myself. With the exception of the Intro to Engineering course, I was averaging a C- in my classes.

I had never done so poorly and I started to worry about failing. However, I visualized two things that gave me a second wind: first, the great disappointment on my mom's face when I told her I was going to drop out of college, and second, not becoming an astronaut. About that time, I stopped working nights, got a tutor and joined study groups. One of my study groups was like a team from the United Nations. Joining me were a Vietnamese-American, a Saudi Arabian and a Venezuelan. We became good friends.

With this help, I recovered and finished my first semester with a B average. The second semester was not any easier because I had Calculus II, Physics I, Elec-

trical Science and Psychology. It seemed that each
semester included one class that gave me trouble. The
previous semester it was Chemistry, and second semester it was Physics. My self-confidence was shaken but I
decided to face my demons head-on. I started sitting in
the front row of the class, asking questions and going to
the professor's office prepared with specific questions
about his lectures. I developed a good relationship with
my physics professor, Dr. Andrés Rodríguez, who was a
short Cuban man who always had an unlit cigar in his
mouth. Dr. Rodríguez knew I was struggling and
warned me that the physics courses weeded out "the
wannabe" engineers from the real engineers.

One day during his office hours, Dr. Rodríguez
smiled and said, "I know you are struggling in my
class, but I can see you're a very hard worker."

"Well, yes . . . " I murmured.

"José, I have complete faith in you. I'm sure you'll
do just fine in my class."

He was right: I earned a B+ and had an overall
average of 3.2 for all my classes that second semester.

As part of the Engineering program at the University
of the Pacific, I had to participate in what was called a
co-op assignment to work as an intern at a company.
The company that interested me the most was
Lawrence Livermore National Laboratory, partly
because its focus was on basic science research and
development. After a stressful interview for the job, I

received a letter accepting me for my first co-op assignment. And they were going to pay me, so I did not have to go back to the fields for summer work. How great was that?

CHAPTER 8

Never Giving Up

The euphoria of getting to work and learn at Lawrence Livermore National Laboratory was short-lived, because the financial aid office at Pacific decided to reduce the financial support they were giving me by the amount of money I would make from Lawrence Livermore. Even worse, Pacific was going to charge me full tuition during the semester I was on my co-op assignment. *Very unfair,* I thought. Nonetheless, I was still happy to have landed my first co-op. More than 12,000 people worked at the Livermore facility with approximately 120 college students from universities across the United States. Lawrence Livermore organized programs such as speakers, tours, barbecues and outings to various places, including Lawrence Berkeley Laboratory on the University of California-Berkeley campus. The fact that the Pacific co-op program stretched our engineering curriculum from the traditional four years to five years seemed be a good trade off. It allowed us aspiring engineers to work with career engineers, obtain valuable work experience and learn what real engineering was about. I did so well during my co-op assignment that I was invited back by the lab for a second assignment.

Flight Day 6

Flight Day 6 consisted of more joint crew operations, including the major task of continuing to empty out the MPLM that had more than seven tons of equipment. Other members of the joint crew continued the activation of the new crew quarters. It was also a day filled with public relations events. Danny Olivas and I were in high demand for news interviews because this was the first time two Hispanic Americans formed part of the same space shuttle crew. I was also sought after by the Spanish-language media and even was interviewed live by one of the national news television shows in Mexico City. I remember that they were very excited that I was tweeting in Spanish and said they were talking each day on the news show about our mission and, in particular, every tweet I was posting.

Once we finished with the day's activities, it was once again time to prep the second team to work outside the station. As they went over the procedures with Mission Control in Houston, a couple of us made sure we staged the suits, helmets, gloves, boots and tools they would need for the spacewalk on Day 7.

Flight Day 7

The day started with Danny Olivas and Christer Fuglesang, an astronaut from Sweden, performing the second spacewalk of the STS-128 mission. Danny and Christer, with the help of the ISS robotic arm that both

Kevin and I operated during their spacewalk, completed the replacement of the Ammonia Tank Assembly (ATA) with a new one. The ATA that the pair had moved weighed 1,800 lbs., the most mass moved by astronauts to date. Once they had installed it, Danny and Christer moved on to other tasks, while the ground operations integrated the newly installed ATA into the cooling loop system. The other tasks they completed included installing protective lens covers and cameras on the same ISS Remote Manipulator System they utilized earlier in the walk, which we simply call the ISS robotic arm. While Danny and Christer were outside, we were busily moving ahead with the transfer of items to and from the shuttle middeck. This second spacewalk lasted six hours and thirty-nine minutes.

Flight Day 8

Our duties on Flight Day 8 were light in comparison to our previous days. The first part of the day we were off duty, which meant we had free time to do personal housekeeping, take personal photographs and, in my case, enjoy the experience. We were more than halfway through our mission, and I still couldn't believe I was up in space. I would never get tired of floating around and propelling myself like Superman. I took photographs for my family as I propped myself against the window with Earth in the background. I also took "hero" shots with items I had brought onboard, including an Oakland Raiders flag.

The NASA Public Affairs Office also had us scheduled for a joint crew photo session and news conference. Later that day, we continued with the daily chore of transferring items out of and into the MPLM while the station crew calibrated the H2 sensor on the Oxygen Generation System. Tim Kopra continued to hand off his space station duties to the new expedition crewmember, Nicole Stott. Once again, we began prepping the space suits for Danny and Christer to work outside the station one last time on Flight Day 9. This would be the longest of the three spacewalks. After dinner, Christer and Danny prepped themselves to spend the night in the sealed Quest Airlock. Once we had them nicely sealed there, we turned in to get some rest.

Another long but fulfilling day in space, I thought, as I rolled out my sleeping bag, tied the four corners to structures and gracefully slid in for some well-deserved rest. As I floated there in my sleeping bag, I started thinking about the first day I was able to officially call myself an engineer.

Graduation day arrived at University of the Pacific in May of 1985, and I was very excited that my undergraduate career was finally coming to a successful end. Even though making the transition from high school to university had been difficult, I found myself graduating "Cum Laude," which is Latin for "With Honors." My parents beamed with pride when they saw me in my cap and gown. I had placed a sign on the top of my graduation cap that read "Thanks Mom!" I was also happy that the Lawrence Livermore National Laboratory had extended me an offer to work there as an engineer, full-time with an incredible salary. Nevertheless, I had a conflict. The University of California at Santa Barbara had accepted me into their Electrical Engineering Graduate Program with a full scholarship. Then I learned that the national laboratory had played a role in selecting me for this scholarship and wanted me to have that great opportunity to study at one of the best Engineering graduate programs.

Graduate school at the University of California, Santa Barbara was one of the best experiences of my life. It was the first time I did not have to work and go to school. My scholarship stipend paid for graduate student housing in an apartment I shared with two other students who had also graduated from Pacific. I even had money left over to pay for my books and food. Classes were hard, but I had all the time in the world to dedicate to my studies, and this made a world of difference. I graduated with honors again and developed great friendships with both students and professors. When I graduated from the Master's program, I received a job offer from Lawrence Livermore that included a substantial raise.

When I returned to the lab, I was assigned to the Chemistry and Material Science Group managed by my former boss, Mike. I went to work immediately on the lab's x-ray laser program, which was developing an x-ray laser to be deployed in space to disable incoming Soviet nuclear missiles in the event of a first strike—we were still in the Cold War. I was happy to work on this program because it involved space. It was a high-profile and high-priority project for which I helped develop methods to evaluate materials with novel imaging techniques. However, about five years into the program, in 1991, the Soviet Union collapsed. When the Cold War was over, so was the justification for expensive projects like the x-ray laser program.

With the end of big projects like this, there was concern about the future of national laboratories, especially the ones dedicated to nuclear defense, such as Lawrence Livermore and Los Alamos National Laboratory in New Mexico. So, we started working on ways to transfer the knowledge we had gained in wartime to peacetime efforts. Our new mission was to partner with private industry and make American companies more competitive in global markets.

The deputy program manager of the x-ray laser program, Clint Logan, and I honed-in on the process we had used for evaluating the materials used to build the x-ray laser. We thought this could be applied to medical imaging. We did some research and convinced ourselves that we had the technology not only to build a better system for x-rays to detect breast cancer, but also we could convert the process from the old film/screen system to producing digital images. Laura Mascio, a bio-med engineer at the lab, completed the team and led in the development of the computer-aided diagnosis software. The team was small but effective.

Everyone knew that the earlier cancer was detected, the greater the chances were for the person to be cured, and our system proposed to do just that. Clint and I wrote a proposal to develop the technology and were given $6 million to work with Fisher Imaging, a small company in Denver. The results were better than we had ever imagined. We were able to put a digital mammography system called Senoscan in the marketplace, and this helped Fisher Imaging earn $100 million a year in sales.

Our project was the poster child of the technology transfer community and brought the laboratory some well-needed positive press. Once the project ended, I was promoted to a management role. I was offered Mike's old position as group leader of the Chemistry and Material Sciences Group, and I accepted it. I led some forty engineers and technicians in environmental sciences, weapons and lasers, among other programs. I enjoyed working as a manager and helping to develop the careers of people in my group, but I also missed being down in the trenches and doing the technical work. I thought to myself that I was still too young to make this management career path permanent. After about two years on the job, I finally found the right opportunity to return to technical work.

At the Lawrence Livermore National Laboratory, we became highly involved in the US-Russia program to convert the highly enriched uranium in Russia's nuclear bombs to peaceful uses, such as fuel for nuclear reactors. After the Cold War, there was no reason for Russia—or the United States for that matter—to have so many nuclear bombs, and I was recruited to join the team that converted megatons of enriched uranium to mega-watts of energy. After being the lead scientist for Lawrence Livermore National Laboratory and having been on approximately a dozen trips to the four main Russian nuclear facilities in Siberia, I was recruited for a related effort in Washington, DC. The job required a two-year commitment to work out of Washington, at the US Department of Energy headquarters.

CHAPTER 9

Getting So Close

We packed our bags and our family moved to the nation's capital. The program I was recruited for was part of the US Department of Energy: the Materials Protection, Control and Accountability Program in the US Department of Energy had the mission, to help them secure their nuclear material stockpile. It involved working with the them at their nuclear facilities and installing high-tech monitoring systems so that the Russians would have complete control of their nuclear materials. We were achieving two main goals in working with the Russians during this era of transition. First, we were making it a lot more difficult for weapons-grade material to make it into the hands of unfriendly nations and terrorist groups. Second, we helped keep the Russian engineers and scientists gainfully employed so they would not be recruited or tempted to offer their expertise to others outside their country.

Flight Day 9

I realized Flight Day 9 was the beginning of the end of our fourteen-day mission. The last spacewalk was scheduled for that day, during which Danny and Christer would install two GPS antennas, deploy the new Starboard Payload Attach System, Rate Gyro Assembly and route the Node 3 avionics cables. Although they had other major responsibilities during our mission, the work outside the station, in space, was by far the most complex and dangerous. Everyone was relieved when they finished. The joint crew of the station and the shuttle also continued with the transfer and installation of equipment, except on Day 9 the focus was on transferring items no longer used on the space station, such as used equipment, experiments, clothes and trash. As the day of our departure drew near, I noticed that we had begun to eat in larger and larger groups, which included members of both the shuttle and space station. I also found I had a greater appreciation for being in space. Perhaps this was because I had become more efficient in navigating through the station and the shuttle, or that I was finding more time to stare out the windows to gaze in amazement at our beautiful planet which we rotated around every ninety minutes. Whatever it was, that was the first day I felt I had the chance to take a moment to soak it all in.

Flight Day 10

On Flight Day 10 our responsibilities were relatively light. The main activities consisted of transferring
frozen experiment samples from the station to the Gla-
cier freezer in the shuttle. Results from these experiments would help scientists develop ways to prevent
the bone density loss and the muscle atrophy that
occurs during long-duration space missions. It was
also the last day for transferring items in and out of the
Leonardo Multi-Purpose Logistics Module. On Day
11, we would complete the closeout procedure of the
module, and close its hatch so that we could transfer it
back to the shuttle's payload bay via the robotic arm. I
was very excited because the bulk of the responsibility
for operating the robotic arm was mine.

The Department of Energy moved my family and
me to the Washington, DC area. We chose to live in
Maryland, where there was an excellent school dis-
trict. The oldest of our four kids, Julio, was starting elementary school. Two weeks after settling into my daily
commute to downtown DC via the Metro subway, I
received a letter from NASA. Unlike the previous five
rejection letters, it advised me that NASA would be
taking a closer look at my application. The letter stated
that approximately three hundred applicants would
go through the screening process and that out of these

one hundred would be selected to be on the shortlist for selection as an astronaut!

I was excited to still be in the running this time, considering that there had been more than 14,000 applicants. This was my sixth year applying and NASA was finally taking notice of me. Two months later, I received a phone call from the Astronaut Selection Office and then a letter confirming that I had passed to the next round in the selection process. I had made it to the final one hundred candidates! I was to be in one of five groups of twenty who would spend one week at the NASA Johnson Space Center in Houston, Texas. During that week, we would be subjected to physical, aptitude and psychological tests and interviews. In between the testing, we would tour the NASA facilities and visit the astronauts to get better insight into what being an astronaut actually entailed.

When my week at NASA arrived, I showed up on a Sunday at NASA's Johnson Space Center, located in the Clear Lake area of Houston. That Monday morning, all twenty candidates met formally and were given a briefing on the week's activities. Everything went pretty well, although I found the psychological test to be too long and repetitive. It contained well over 1,400 questions and lasted over four hours. The physical was also very detailed.

The only area where I struggled a bit was the depth perception eye test, which consisted of staring through an apparatus that looked like a microscope, called a depth perception vision screener, with which you had to look through the eyepieces at five circles and tell the optometrist which circle was out-of-plane. I remember when I first stared at it I could not distinguish the out-of-plane circle and started to panic. They had told us at the briefing that on average 20% of the candidates interviewed were disqualified for physical or medical reasons. The optometrist was extremely nice and told me to do a fuzzy focus, take deep breaths and relax. After about five minutes, I started to identify the out-of-plane circle, and I was able to run through the sequence of circles. "OK, you nailed them," he announced, to my relief. *That was a very close call,* I thought.

I went through the rest of the tests that week with no noticeable problems and closed out the week with the interview. The interview panel consisted of eighteen individuals, including astronauts, managers and administrators from NASA headquarters in Washington, DC. The discussion was free-flowing, as they encouraged you to talk about yourself. The hour seemed to go by a lot faster than I had imagined.

Once all five groups of twenty were interviewed, the waiting game began. It would be an indefinite amount of time before we got the results. It was not until six or seven months after the last group was interviewed that the calls to the group finally started to come in. I had not been selected. But they did tell me that I was a strong candidate and should keep applying. I was very disappointed. On a follow-up call with the head of the Astronaut Selection Office, Duane Ross, he told me that the main issue was I was unknown and lacked operational experience. It would help, he said, if I took a job at NASA's Johnson Space Center in Houston. In essence, I was being offered a consolation prize. He did emphasize, however, that if I accepted the job, it in no way would guarantee that I would be invited to be a finalist. In other words, every year my application would be thrown into the big pile and would have to make the cut on merit. The job offer was for work in the engineering department. I explained to Duane that I could not take the job right away because I had made a two-year commitment to the Department of Energy. I ended the conversation saying that I hoped it would not hurt my chances during the selection of the next class of astronauts.

Back at my job in Washington, DC, I continued traveling to the Siberian countryside. Before long, I was a few months away from completing my two-year assignment, and my wife Adelita and I looked forward to moving back to California. Being away from our families was difficult, especially with four little ones who missed their grandparents. Out of the blue, I received another letter from NASA informing me that I once again was one of the one hundred finalists. Again, I was given the date of my interview week. This time, I approached it much more cautiously and lowered my expectations, remembering my previous experience and the devastation I felt when I was not selected. Once again, I visited Johnson Space Center and went through a similar series of tests and exams. When the day of the phone calls came, I was informed that I had not been selected. I was disappointed, but this time I took it a lot better. When Duane Ross made a follow-up call, he again stressed the importance of taking a job at Johnson Space Center.

If I accepted the job at NASA in Houston, I would be earning 10-to-15% less than my current salary. It was a difficult choice for my family and me to make. I knew that if I did not accept the NASA job offer, I was more than likely not going to be considered in future selections. *Life is about taking calculated risks,* I thought.

However, it was a family decision, not just mine. My conversation with my wife went surprisingly well. She had brothers not too far from Houston, in Port Arthur, Texas, and did not feel she would be alone in Texas. She was also not worried about the cut in pay; she had always handled our family budget with care. It was decided: instead of moving back to California, we would move to Houston, Texas!

Flight Day 11

We finally finished transferring and installing some 7 tons of equipment to the space station. It was time to deactivate the Multi-purpose Logistics Module (MPLM), close its hatch, de-mate it and berth it back in the shuttle's payload bay. I was the principal robotic arm operator responsible for that task. Being the main operator is a huge task, as you are often operating the arm in the blind and relying on cameras for clearance verification. This is why the arm is always operated by two persons, the principal operator and the person that backs you up on all your maneuvers. A very stressful but rewarding experience! Once I finished, I joined Nicole Stott and took part in a public affairs event that involved live interviews.

Because we were so busy with our timelines, we usually ate in groups of three or four. But that last night, both crews got together for a large meal. We all shared our Russian- and American-prepared foods. The Russians stored their food in cans, so they were able to offer us various meats and fish. We shared with them our ready-to-eat meal pouches, including shrimp cocktail, chicken with rice and strawberries and cream for dessert. After dinner, we had a farewell ceremony.

Then, the space station crew that now included Nicole Stott closed their hatch. We did the same and depressurized Mating Adapter 2. The final activity of the day was for me to check the rendezvous tools on the portable on-board computers to ensure they were ready to use first thing the next morning.

Flight Day 12

Flight Day 12 was especially important. We successfully undocked from the International Space Station and slowly but surely backed away from it. The two pilots at the controls fired the Reaction Control System Jets, while I watched the screen visuals and called out rates, speeds, distances and trajectory information. Just as docking at the International Space Station had been challenging, this maneuver took quite a bit of time and concentration from all members of the crew. To add to the complexity of the maneuver, the commander and pilot not only had to undock and back away to a safe distance, but also had to perform a 360-degree fly around of the space station. This was done so that we could take high-resolution pictures of all angles of the station and enable engineers on the ground to inspect for any exterior damage just as the station crew had done for our shuttle as we docked.

After the fly around, the pilots performed two separation burns, using the Reaction Control System thrusters. Shortly after these burns, and being a safe distance from the space station, Kevin, Christer and I connected the shuttle's robotic arm to the Orbital Boom Sensor System and began the final inspection of our Thermal Protection System.

CHAPTER 10

Getting the Call

After the school year was complete, we finally moved into our new house in the Clear Lake, a suburb next to the Johnson Space Center. We moved in on June 6, 2001, the same day that Tropical Storm Allison hit. Allison circled continuously around the Houston area, causing widespread flooding. I remember waking up the next morning to find our streets under water. Our home was slightly elevated, and Allison dumped enough water to cover the third and final step of our walkway from the street to our house. It came dangerously close to flooding our newly bought house. Phew! That was a close call.

We quickly settled into a routine at our new home, and I started working at Johnson Space Center's Engineering's Materials and Processes branch. The technical work was a welcome change; it had been a few years since I had worked on evaluating materials that fail in operation. To do so, I had to use ultrasound, x-ray imaging, scanning electron microscopes and other tools and techniques. I worked with a great group of NASA engineers and technicians dedicated to human space flight. Their dedication would be put to the test, as I was about to find out.

After about eight months on the job, I became the acting chief of the branch, leading a group of forty scientists, engineers and technicians. Everything was going great until one fateful Saturday morning. I was watching TV at home, when there was a report that something had gone wrong with Space Shuttle Columbia. She was completing her space flight mission and was due to come home that day. I was in shock: a catastrophic failure had occurred! TV images showed Columbia breaking into pieces somewhere over northern Texas.

I headed straight to my NASA office where, little by little, my branch members gathered in our conference room. Together, we watched news updates. Later that day, people began to be deployed to various parts of northern Texas and Louisiana to begin the process of collecting the thousands of pieces of the shattered shuttle. Needless to say, all seven crewmembers died during the accident. Soon, a hangar with the shuttle's outline on the floor was set up to reconstruct the accident. Our engineering department worked on two major fronts of the investigation: first, the evaluation of key pieces of the shuttle and, second, the re-creation of the cause of the accident. We suspected that a piece of insulating foam from the external tank had come off and hit the leading edge of the wing, causing enough damage that upon re-entry of the shuttle, hot plasma had made its way into the internal frame of the wing and caused the catastrophic failure. The front portion of a shuttle wing was built to exact specifications, and a similar size piece of foam that was captured on video falling off the external tank and impacting the wing was shot using a high-speed air canon. After repeated tests, we demonstrated that hot plasma had gone through the wing's carbon composite material and caused the damage. We had gotten to the root cause through sophisticated engineering tests.

Months later, NASA announced that it would pick another class of astronauts. NASA had not picked a new class in four years; it was a long time coming. I was fortunate enough to, once again, make the final list of one hundred candidates. It would be my third time, my twelfth application to date. NASA does not discriminate with respect to age, but I knew there was a practical age at which NASA would stop inviting me to be a candidate. *I was already forty-one years old, so it was now or never,* I thought. During my interview week, I went through a process that was all-too-familiar. Many people on the selection board knew me because I had either provided them with engineering support or had reported to them on the results of the Columbia accident investigation. I finished the week with a lot of optimism, but quickly dove back into my duties as branch chief.

A few months passed, and I got so involved in my job that I hardly thought about my astronaut candidacy. Then, the big day finally arrived. I was sitting in my office when I received a call from Johnson Space Center Director, Bob Cabana, an astronaut himself. He made small talk and then asked a question that immediately made me realize this was the call I had been waiting for all my life.

"José, are you replaceable as the branch chief?"

"Everyone is replaceable, Bob. If I've been doing my job correctly in mentoring a few members of my branch, a transition should be seamless."

He must have liked the answer because he said, "Good, because I would like to welcome you to the astronaut corps."

I was glad I was sitting down, because my legs felt wobbly and I was speechless!

"Okay, then," Director Cabana said. "But you have to promise not to tell anyone until the official announcement, next month, in May."

"Well, can I at least tell my wife and parents?"

"Only if they can keep a secret."

After gathering my composure, I left the office, got in my car and drove home. On my 8-minute ride home I had the radio on and the song "Don't Stop Believing" by Journey played. Later in my career I would not only be interviewed with Journey on Oprah, but would incorporate this song as part of my motivational talks. I had to tell Adelita in person and call my parents in California. When I entered the house, my wife thought I was coming home early for lunch. I gave her the great news and we hugged and cried. Then we called my parents. It felt so good to share this with them. They had not let me give up on my dream. Adelita had followed me to Washington, DC, then to Houston and had sacrificed so much to get us to this point. My parents had given me the license to dream big. They had given me the recipe for success and provided a nurturing environment that allowed me to thrive in school.

Flight Day 13

I could hardly believe we were beginning our thirteenth day in space; it felt like we had just arrived. There we were, the seven of us who had spent the better part of two years training for that mission, sharing the same office and interacting with each other's families. *We were a tight-knit group, and it was about to end,* I thought. The only difference on our return was that Nicole Stott would be staying behind as part of the space station crew and Tim Kopra would be returning home with us after his three months there.

On Day 13, our commander CJ and pilot Kevin performed standard checks of the Flight Control System, the Reaction Control and the air-to-ground communication system. We deactivated the camera system used to inspect the thermal protection system on the shuttle's underbelly, nose cone and leading edges of the wings. We also stowed the Ku-band antenna that deployed externally on our first day of flight and that had been used for some of our communications. The last part of our day was spent reviewing landing procedures and taking quick looks at the weather forecast for our landing. Things did not look good at Kennedy Space Center: there was a low cloud ceiling and an 80% chance of thunderstorms. Although the possibility of landing on Day 14 at our scheduled time did not look good, we still had to press on and assume the weather would improve for us to land. Toward the end of the day, we had a little free time to film each other and take more hero shots. We also played with our food and filmed how water behaves in free-floating space.

Flight Day 14

Our final day in space arrived all too soon. Discovery was scheduled to land at Kennedy Space Center at 19:04 EDT, but just as the weather forecast had predicted, the landing was postponed due to unfavorable weather conditions. Flight rules called for us to orbit once more around the Earth and wait for a second opportunity to see if the weather conditions improved. Our new landing time was 20:40 EDT. Unfortunately, the weather still did not cooperate, and our landing had to be delayed by one day. This gave us an extra day in space. With most of our things stowed for landing, ground control could not come up with enough chores to keep us fully occupied. This gave us plenty of time to reflect on our experience in space and truly appreciate it. We continued taking photos of ourselves and filming "What if in microgravity we do this?" types of experiments. After our fun day in space, we got ready for bed. I started to think about how well our mission had gone as a result of being well-trained during the past eighteen months and what a long but enjoyable journey my life had been to this point.

CHAPTER 11

The Training Begins

We were introduced to the public on May 6, 2004, as the nineteenth class of astronauts. Each class had their name, and ours was the Peacocks. According to tradition, the previous classes had to approve of the name, so it could not be too flashy, like the Hawks or the Eagles. The class of 1996 was named the Sardines and the 1998 class was the Penguins, because the Sardines were a large class and few thought the Penguin class would fly in space due to the uncertainty of the space program. We were called the Peacocks because peacocks are birds that are all-show and can barely fly. We were not crazy about the name, but it could have been worse. They could have called us Dodos, an extinct, flightless bird!

That summer, we all reported to Johnson Space Center for a one-week briefing and in-depth tours of the manned spaceflight training facilities. We were also taken to Ellington Air Field, where NASA has about twenty-eight T-38 trainer jets, which are part of NASA's continuous training curriculum; astronaut candidates had to fly a minimum number of hours as pilots and flight engineers to get accustomed to working together as a team of two crewmembers.

When we arrived at Ellington Field, we were all issued our NASA blue flight suits and jackets. I remember going home that day excited to try them on. I looked at myself in my wife's full-body mirror and tried to figure out what all the zippers and pockets were for. As I was savoring the moment, my five-year-old daughter, Yesenia Marisol, walked into the bedroom. I expected her to say something to the effect that I was her hero, now that I was an astronaut. She tilted her head one way and gave me a puzzled look. She raised her arm and pointed her index finger at me, and announced, "Daddy, you look like Papa Smurf!" In one single comment, Yesi had brought me back down to Earth! I am so grateful that my kids, wife, parents and brothers and sister have always kept me grounded and have never let me forget where I come from.

Shortly after our orientation, the whole class was shipped to Pensacola, Florida, for a condensed flight-training course with T-34C turbo prop planes. Before we got into the planes, we had to go through basic survival training, including water survival and parachuting. After that, we trained as flight engineer pilots on the T-34C.

Although the workload was heavy, I did not find things difficult. But water survival training was something else. I had never taken formal swimming lessons, and one of the first exercises was treading water in our flight gear for a certain amount of time. Believe me, when you have heavy boots, helmet and flight suit weighing you down, you have to work hard to stay afloat. We had Chris, a Navy Seal, in our class, and he of course made it look effortless. After treading water came the challenge of swimming in gear a certain distance within a specific amount of time. Again, it was a challenge for me. I have to admit, I was in the last group to finish—although I am proud to say, I was not the last person!

The biggest challenge was the helio dunker exercise, which required six of us to get into the carcass of a helicopter fuselage and strap ourselves in a five-point harness. The helio dunker would then slowly be submerged in fifteen feet of water; right before it reached the bottom, it would rotate 180 degrees, leaving us to land on the bottom of the pool upside down! It was only then that we were allowed to unbuckle and take one of the three exits available and swim to the surface still in our flight gear. Obviously, we had to hold our breaths during this whole process, and there were safety divers to help us in the event we got into trouble, and to ensure that we did not cheat and unbuckle before we were allowed to do so. We did this once and then a second time, when we had to crisscross each other and work as a team to coordinate our exits. We were so excited when we finished this part of the exercise.

Then it was announced that there would be a third and final helio dunk. This time the instructors gave each of us a pair of swimming goggles that had been painted black! We had to feel our way out of the submerged helio! After barely negotiating that exercise successfully, we were done with surviving in the water. Thank goodness!

We returned to Johnson Space Center and went through the rest of the eighteen-month curriculum, which in part involved flying the NASA T-38 jet trainers. Although I had experience flying a Cessna 152, I quickly learned that things in a jet happened much faster. Communication with air traffic control and the tower had to be brief and specific. That is when I learned what they meant by "operations experience." As an engineer, you always want to know why and how everything works. In the operations world, you need to perform the procedure without over-analyzing it, and this, I have to admit, took me a while to learn. Despite this, I got the flight training necessary to be an effective back-seat flight engineer. Soon we were flying with astronaut pilots once or twice a week to complete the required flight hours.

While we were at Ellington Field for flight training, we also dove into academic training. We took courses on the various systems of the space shuttle, including hydraulics, electrical, flight control, avionics, communications and auxiliary power, to name a few. Each week we had written tests; it was like being in final exams on

a continuous basis. At the same time, we also had sim-
ulation training. At first, it was single-system training in
which we were exposed to failures—electrical one
week, then hydraulic the next week, and so on. Then we
moved on to multi-system training, which involved
learning the effects of one-system failures on other systems. Finally, we moved on to the high-fidelity motion-
based training, for which we formed a pick-up crew of
four who took turns being the commander, pilot, MS-1
or MS-2. Each had distinct responsibilities during the
simulations in handling the presented failures. We simulated ascents, on-orbit operations and landings.

Upon completing the shuttle academic training,
we started academic training for the International
Space Station, followed by space station simulations.
After the eighteen months, we were ready for finals,
which included written tests, orals and full-fledged
simulations. We had to pass everything in order to get
our wings and be eligible for a flight assignment. The
training teams did an outstanding job; we all earned
our wings. Our families came to the Johnson Space
Center and witnessed us getting our silver astronaut
pins. In the future, some of us would get a gold astronaut pin after having returned from a space mission.

After the pinning ceremony, we were given technical assignments in support of space missions, while
continuing to participate in pick-up crew simulations,
ISS training and flying T-38s. Everyone got one major
assignment and one minor assignment. My major

assignment was to be part of a four-astronaut team called Astronaut Support Personnel. The minor assignment was to represent the Astronaut Office at the Portable On-board Computer Configuration Board. Our astronaut support job was to prepare the inside portion of the space shuttle before each launch and configure the cockpit in accordance with the flight requirements. That consisted of attending many meetings to gather the information necessary to meet mission requirements. About four months before launch, we would have a practice run at the launch pad at Kennedy Space Center, and two months before the launch, we would have a full dress rehearsal with the crew. Finally, about one week before the launch, we would again fly to the Cape, begin final preparations for the real launch and await the crew's arrival.

Being a member of the astronaut support team meant long hours and plenty of travel. With this assignment, I was right in the middle of the action; it allowed me to gain valuable operations experience. We traveled to the Kennedy Space Center so often that we had our own personal rooms there, decorated with family photos and with a small wardrobe of civilian clothes.

I participated in six launches before being assigned to my first mission. In the email welcoming me to the STS-128 mission, the crew commander, CJ, specified that the mission had three main objectives. First, we would do a crew exchange, with Nicole Stott transferring to the space station and Tim Kopra coming home with us. Second, we would take up more than seven tons of equipment. Third, we would conduct three spacewalks to install some of the equipment on the exterior of the space station and do preparatory plumbing and wiring work for a soon-to-be-installed module.

Right before training was to begin, we received an email from CJ giving us our crew assignments. I was relieved to have not been assigned to walk in space, which was not my strongest suit. Instead, I was fortunate to have been named the MS-2 flight engineer, a very dynamic position that worked very closely with both the commander and the pilot. Each of the crewmembers trained in their specific chores for launch, flight, docking with the space station, carrying out our individual and group duties and re-entry. Among the specific tasks that Kevin and I had were prepping the astronauts for their spacewalks and checking their life support system.

Training for our fourteen-day mission took us eighteen months to complete. There was a lot to learn, most of which we learned through simulated ascent/entry runs, on-orbit operations and spacewalks. As our training continued and we got more proficient, the training team took pride in simulating difficult failures that could occur, especially during ascent and re-entry where our reaction time was critical. The only problem was that they piled up the failures so that we had to be quick and recognize the effects of the system failures on the other systems. For example, they would fail one of the three main engines and, depending on the time of failure, we would have to decide if the remaining two engines would have enough thrust to reach low orbit and then perform an abort or a transatlantic landing in Europe or, worst-case scenario, return to the launch site. As if this problem was not serious enough, they would add an electrical bus failure and landing gear hydraulic failure, followed by the failure of an auxiliary power unit. In short, the training crew would typically throw the kitchen sink at us to prepare us for the worst possible scenarios.

It was July of 2009, and as the launch date approached, we felt more ready than ever. There were three rookies on this mission; Nicole, Kevin and myself, and we were equally excited knowing that in a few short weeks we would all be in space on a rendezvous with the International Space Station. In short, I could not believe that I was about to realize my life-long dream.

Flight Day 15

The final day arrived all too quickly, and we once again began initial preparations for landing. The weather forecast was again not too favorable. This time, I was hoping the weather would cooperate because I preferred to land at Kennedy Space Center since our families were ready to give us a hero's welcome there. Any more delays and we would be looking at landing at our second or third preferred landing sites. After finding out that the weather was once again going to be an issue, ground control decided that we would land at our secondary site: Edwards Air Force Base in Southern California.

We began our fluid load protocol, which called for each crewmember to drink a large amount of fluids in the form of water, chicken broth or something that tasted like a poor version of Gatorade. Salt tablets were also part of this protocol. Fluid loading is necessary, because the body loses excess fluids, mainly from the legs, when in a microgravity environment. However, upon returning to the 1-G environment of Earth, the body needs these fluids to minimize the effect of 1-G adaptation sickness, which is the opposite of space sickness.

CJ and Kevin loaded the target information onto the flight computers in preparation for our new landing site. At 19:37 EDT, the pilots initiated Discovery's de-orbit burn, which slowed down the shuttle to the point that the Earth's atmosphere captured it, thus initiating its descent. It was at that point that we reached Mach 25, which meant we were entering the planet at twenty-five times the speed of sound. On land, we would receive Mach 25 patches to sew onto our blue flight suits.

Re-entry, as compared to our blastoff, was anti-climactic for me. I did feel my helmet getting heavy as we went from zero to one G, but the ride was not too bad. There was turbulence that I would describe as bad, but no worse than you would experience flying over the Rockies on a hot summer afternoon. Halfway through the flight, things got smoother, so smooth that it felt like a regular plane ride. As we followed our landing procedures, CJ lined us up with Runway 22L, approaching at a 19-degree angle before performing the flair maneuver that brought up the nose of the shuttle. Kevin checked the landing gear isolation valve per my queue and initiated landing gear deployment. CJ did a great job of landing the shuttle safely and smoothly at 20:53 EDT (17:53 PDT). The parachute that was supposed to deploy as soon as we landed to slow down the shuttle and act as a brake was delayed per Mission Control Instructions and, shortly after deployment, CJ applied the pedal brakes to come to a full stop.

When CJ announced, "Wheels stop," our STS-128 space mission had ended. Then, ground control sent a message: "Congratulations, Discovery, on a successful mission, and thanks for stepping up science."

We had made it home to Earth, but it would take between 45 minutes and an hour before the hatch

would open up and one of our colleagues would
unstrap us and take us down to the Astrovan. It was
about 6:00 pm, and we were in the Mojave dessert.
The temperature was quickly warming up. When I
raised or turned my head to flip switches, things got
blurry for a few seconds. It was a dizzying side effect.

Soon after we finished our procedures, a support
astronaut opened the hatch and welcomed us home.
He first let the middeck crew out: Danny, Christer and
Tim. After they safely entered the Astrovan, the support team came back for the flight deck crew, and I
was the first to be unstrapped, then Pat, then Kevin
and finally CJ. Once we were all in the Astrovan, our
commander gave each of us a high five and congratu-
lated us all on a job well done. He indicated he was
proud of each and every one of us and that he would
be honored if we ever flew together again.

The suit technicians began to take off our orange
flight suits. To take these off, you have to duck your
head in and come out the backside. My shoulders are
somewhat broad, and I was unsuccessful in egressing
from the backside on the first try; I struggled so much
that I had to pop my head back up for fresh air. I tried
it a second time and struggled, but finally managed to
come out of the suit. At that point, I was hot, clammy
and dizzy and had to ask for a bag to throw up in. I
felt bad for about five-to-ten minutes, but breathing
the cool, air-conditioned air helped. I guessed that I
was suffering from "1-G adaptation sickness."

Once we stepped out of the Astrovan to greet people and get on the van that would take us to the medical office, I noticed my legs and balance were still shaky. I had to take somewhat of a cowboy stance to combat the lack of balance. We would spend about an hour getting a check up and donating samples of blood and urine at the medical office. We were all released and sent to our accommodations at the base for that evening. We were informed that we would fly back to Ellington Field the following day, where we would be reunited with our families. It was early evening, and CJ suggested we all go out to dinner with the support team to Domingo's, a Mexican restaurant located in the nearby town of Boron, California. It felt good to eat normal food and have a cold beer.

CHAPTER 12

Coming Home

After waking up the next day, I still felt the effects of having spent fourteen days in space. The scenery kept rolling in front of me after sudden turns of my head, and my balance was still not at 100%. Our flight home the following day seemed short compared to the flight we had just completed. We arrived at Ellington Field that afternoon and made our way into the T-38 jet hangar, which was set up with a stage and chairs for about 250 people. Most were employees, media and family members, along with a few autograph seekers.

I was very excited that I was finally going to see my wife, kids and parents. Immediately after getting out of the plane, we were met by our families. The kids ran toward us to give their parents hugs and kisses. My wife, Adelita, and my parents were not far behind my kids. The reunion was brief, because we were expected to go immediately to the stage for the traditional welcome home rally. During the rally, the center director gave his congratulatory remarks, followed by proclamations from local politicians. Next, CJ took to the microphone and gave a summary of our mission, congratulating each crewmember along with the ground folks there at Kennedy Space Center and the mission operation folks in Houston at Johnson Space Center. Each crewmember was given a few minutes on the microphone to describe their individual experiences.

We spent the next few days debriefing and preparing the flight video that would be used to summarize our flight at an upcoming presentation at Space Center Houston in front of family and the Houston community. Those first few evenings at home took some getting used to. I would find myself going outside and looking up at the night sky, thinking that only a few days ago I was up there orbiting our planet every ninety minutes. I also reminisced about what it took to get me there and thought about how important it was that my mother was always on top of our studies and provided that ever-important nurturing home environment that allowed us to thrive in school. I also thought about my father, who only had a third-grade education, but had the wisdom to not only encourage my dream but also to give me the recipe that to this day I still use.

1. Define what you want to do in life.
2. Recognize how far you are from your goal.
3. Draw yourself a roadmap.
4. Prepare yourself with a good education.
5. Develop a good work ethic and always give more than what people expect of you.
6. Perseverance—Never ever give up on yourself!

Later, I thanked Pops for not only giving me the license to dream big but also for giving me the tools, in his recipe, to make that dream a reality. I'm sure things would have been very different had he asked me not to dream so big, for fear of failing and thus becoming disillusioned. I also can't help wondering what our life would have been like had Ms. Young not taken the time to visit my parents and convince them to stay in one place so that our education could gain traction.

Whenever I speak at events where I know teachers will be listening, I always make it a point to tell Ms. Young's story. The moral of the story is that any little thing a teacher does, which she or he may think is insignificant, can change the outcome of a student's life, and their whole family's for that matter. Her impact was so significant that, upon learning of my flight assignment, I added her and her husband to my launch attendee list. I'm happy to say, she accepted my invitation and was standing next to my parents when I blasted off into space. The sixth ingredient, Perseverance, I added to Pops' recipe because NASA rejected me not only once, twice, three or four times, but eleven times! It was not until the twelfth attempt that, in 2004, NASA finally accepted me as part of the nineteenth class of astronauts.

These failures taught me that there are three stages to reaching a goal. Stage One is pretty obvious, so obvious that I think it is human intuition. If one has a goal, the first thing to ask is how do I get there. In other words, what are the minimum requirements? For example, if you want to be a doctor, you know you should perhaps major in pre-med, then certainly go to medical school and then pass your medical boards before you become a practicing physician. If you want to be a lawyer, it's pre-law, law school and then pass the bar exam. If you want to be an astronaut, it is recommended you study in a STEM-related field, go to graduate school and, because it is so competitive, even get a Ph.D. before submitting your first NASA application. Since this stage was obvious, I was already religiously following it.

I remember that about six months after turning in my first application, I received a rejection letter that acknowledged I met the minimum requirements. The issue was that about 14,000 other people also met the minimum requirements. The folks at NASA ended their letter by thanking me and encouraging me to reapply. The letter did not even address me by name, but rather as "Dear Applicant." However, I was proud of that first letter. It had the NASA logo and acknowledged my application, which to me was a good first step. As the years passed and the rejection letters piled up, the feeling soon changed from exuberance to disappointment. Nobody likes rejection, and hearing thanks but no thanks five years in a row wears on a person. I remember thinking that I was never going to be selected. So strong was that feeling that, unlike my first rejection letter, I scrunched this letter into a ball and threw it on the bedroom floor, convinced that it was time to give up the pipe dream of trying to become an astronaut. Five years of trying and not making any progress was enough to convince me that it probably wasn't meant to be.

Lucky for me, though, my wife was cleaning the bedroom later that day and came across the scrunched-up letter. She carefully unraveled it and read it.

Then, she looked for me and asked, "What's this?"

I saw this as an opportunity to score some pity points with her.

"I guess NASA does not want me. I've decided to give up on dreaming about becoming an astronaut." I was expecting her to feel sorry for me and to try to make me feel better.

Instead, Adelita looked at me and asked, "So, you're going to quit on your dream?"

"Well, it's been five years, and all I have to show for it is one rejection letter after another."

"Look, José, I don't see anything in this letter that says NASA wants you to stop applying. They're just saying that in this selection cycle, they are not selecting you. In fact, they end the letter by saying, 'Please feel free to apply again.' José, I know you. I also know that if you give up, you're always going to have that little worm of curiosity inside of you, wondering, 'What if? What if I had applied that seventh, eighth or ninth time?' This doubt will be eating you from the inside, and you're going to become a bitter old man. . . . And guess what? I do not want to be married to a bitter old man. So I suggest you rethink your decision. "

I thought about it a while and concluded that she was right. I needed to see this through and decided to apply once again. But this time I decided to do things a little differently. That's when the Second Stage of reaching a goal became clear to me: Look at people who are already there and ask yourself, "What attributes do they have that I don't?" Be honest with yourself in answering this question. The first time I did that and compared myself with the new class of astronauts, I finally understood. We had similar educational backgrounds and similar work experience. But deep down there were some fundamental differences. All newly selected astronauts were licensed pilots, and I was not. So I started taking flying lessons at a small airport in Tracy, California. Six months later, I was flying solo. I had also found out that all newly selected astronauts were scuba diver rated. So I joined the lab's scuba club and got certified for Basic, Advanced, Scuba Rescue and Master. I wanted to make sure NASA was convinced I knew how to scuba dive!

The Third Stage to reaching your goal is to be strategic and do things that separate you from the competition. In 1998, when I was working at Lawrence Livermore National Lab, one such opportunity arose and I leapt at the chance to work on the Highly Enriched

Uranium Purchase Agreement Program. Quite honestly, I don't think many people were clamoring for the job because it involved quite a bit of travel, weeks at a time, to the nuclear materials processing sites in Siberia. I decided to take the job, not because I was anxious to get to know Siberia in the middle of winter, but because I found out that the United States and the newly formed Russian Federation, along with fourteen other countries, had just signed an agreement to build an International Space Station. I saw it as an opportunity to gain experience few people could get at the time. It would allow me to learn to work with the Russians, learn the Russian culture and, with the blessing of my boss at the lab, take courses in the Russian language to help me do my job effectively. So important was this experience, I thought, that I accepted a two-year stint at the Department of Energy in Washington, DC, in support of another Russia-focused activity: the Materials Protection, Control and Accountability Program. I made sure to highlight these experiences on my NASA astronaut applications.

It took me twelve years to stumble upon the three stages of reaching a goal:

1. Know the requirements
2. Acquire the attributes of successful people you want to emulate
3. Distinguish yourself from the competition

I am thoroughly convinced that these three stages, along with Pop's recipe for success, is the winning formula to reach any goal in life. I hope this formula will save a few years of agony for anyone reading this book, in reaching their personal goals in life. You're never too old to dream, let alone make those dreams a reality.

My fourteen-day mission to space changed my perspective on life in two ways. The first has to do with our environment. Once up in space, I had plenty of opportunity to watch sunsets and sunrises in our 217 revolutions around Earth. I remember one particular sunrise as we were coming from the dark side of the planet. As I watched the sun come up on the horizon, I could clearly see the thickness of our atmosphere. What I saw during those few seconds really surprised me, because the atmosphere looked scarily thin! To think that this is the only thing that is keeping us alive made me an instant environmentalist. I guess I was always conscientious of our environment, but seeing the planet from that perspective made me realize how fragile our planet is and that we should be good stewards of our environment.

Our goal should be to leave planet Earth in as good or better condition than when we arrived, thus ensuring that our children and children's children will enjoy the same quality of life we have today. That day, I promised myself that each time I had an audience, I would bring this particular experience of mine to light in hopes of raising awareness about the delicate nature of our environment.

The second event that changed my outlook on life actually occurred during the first day in space. When we cut off the main engine after 8 minutes and 30 seconds of powered flight, we were officially in space and began orbiting Earth. Since the three members in the middeck had no flight responsibilities during our ascent, they started to unbuckle themselves and reconfigure the middeck, which involved folding and storing our seats, activating the kitchen galley and bathroom and even opening up the payload bay doors.

I remained in my seat assisting the pilots and an hour later, I unbuckled and floated to the middeck. I clumsily made my way to the hatch window in my best Superman impersonation, so that I could see Earth from a new perspective. Approximately five hundred out of the more than seven billion people on Earth have this privilege, and I was determined to make that first look a memorable one.

As I floated to the window, I wondered what I would see and quickly had a flashback of being in Ms. Cotton's fifth grade class, where we were learning world geography. Ms. Cotton would spin a world globe and stop it at a particular country, and then we students had to write down the name of the country and its capital. Obviously, when I reached the hatch window I did not expect to see countries we were flying over in different colors, like on Ms. Cotton's globe, but I did expect to differentiate them quite easily. As we were starting to fly over North and Central America, I saw this amazing view of lots of water, clouds and landmasses. I was breathless, amazed at the beautiful place we humans call home. I was able to recognize Canada, the United States and Mexico, but what struck me the most was that I could not distinguish where Canada ended and the United States began. I also could not differentiate where the United States ended and Mexico began, and so on down through Central America.

I said to myself, "Wow, I had to leave our beautiful planet to realize that down there we are just one." From my perspective up there, there were no borders. It made me realize that humans created borders to separate each other. *How sad,* I thought. Back on Earth, I keep telling people that I wish there was some way to get our world leaders up into space so that they can have this same "Ah-ha" moment. I am willing to bet that upon their return, our world would be a much more peaceful place. Perhaps I'm overly optimistic, but space is truly a remarkable place. It can change the perspective on life and the planet of us who are blessed to have the opportunity to visit.

Afterword

Fatherhood is one of the most challenging and joyful endeavors, a job that never ends and almost has no recipe. Having had the opportunity to spend a few evenings with Pops, it is no wonder that José ended up exploring the final frontier. Becoming an astronaut is no easy task, but the practical, actionable advice his father has given him stands the test of time and is applicable across the board to any professional aspirations that a boy or girl might or could have.

Education is the key, but it takes more than education. As a father (and a mother), you need to prepare your children, and it is more than just education. As you follow José's journey you notice that perseverance, the ability to bounce back stronger from setbacks, is a key ingredient in his recipe to success. As a boy or girl with lofty goals, you need to hone a number of skills to follow the recipe. José had to work on all these skills while he followed his father's recipe to become an astronaut. I refer to these skills as physical, emotional and intellectual fitnesses. The emotional fitness ensured that José was never discouraged or disappointed and had the full support of his family, his parents when he was young and as he got older his very supportive wife Adelita and their children Julio, Karina, Vanessa, Yesenia and Antonio. The intellectual fitness is the education to know your job, to know it well and to be good at what you do. José got to where he is because he excelled at every job he had, and every task he was given, he knocked out of the park. He learned in school, from teachers, mentors, colleagues and even from those who worked for him. Intellectual fitness means that you never stop learning. Finally, physical fitness: you cannot have the endurance you need to do the things worth doing if you are not physically fit. Eat clean, no drugs and take care of yourself. José is an avid runner, and a fast one at that.

In reading this fascinating book, you noticed that José followed Pops' recipe intellectually, emotionally and physically. You too can do that to chart your own course.

My family and I are grateful to call José, Adelita and their children our friends, and we feel blessed to have received the recipe firsthand from Pops.

José, congratulations on an incredible life, a wonderful journey, and thanks for sharing your recipe.

Dr. Gurpartap Sandhoo
Captain, US Navy
Superintendent, Spacecraft Engineering
Department, US Naval Research Laboratory

Glossary

"L Minus 20-Minute" hold—during which the count-down clock stops before liftoff (L), so that NASA controllers and astronauts can conduct final launch team briefings and allow the guidance folks to complete pre-flight alignments that would keep the spacecraft on the desired trajectory throughout the mission.

"L Minus 9-Minute" hold—another built-in delay to make a Go-No-Go decision and make final preparations for launch.

access arm—an enclosed bridge that allows the crew to enter the shuttle through the access hatch (like the air bridge used to board an airplane). It connects the shuttle Discovery to the White Room where the closeout crew help the astronauts get ready.

access hatch—is the entry and exit from the space shuttle, it has a pressurized seal to maintain the air pressure inside the shuttle so that the astronauts can breathe when they remove their space suits.

Advanced Crew Escape Space Suit System (ACES or, the pumpkin suit) also known as the **Launch Entry Suit (LES)** this space suit protects the astronaut during the space shuttle launch and landing in case something goes wrong. The pieces of the suit, including the gloves and helmet, fit together so that none of the astronaut's skin is exposed. The suit is high tech, it provides oxygen for breathing, maintains air pressure, maintains body temperature, and includes tools to help the astronaut escape if necessary (parachute, flotation device, radio, swiss army knife, flare gun, etc . . .)

aero surface profile test—is the moment when the wing flaps and rudder are positioned for launch.

airlock—is an airtight room with two doors that allows the astronaut to go on a spacewalk without letting any of the air out of the space station.

ammonia tank assembly—is a critical component of the International Space Station's (ISS) thermal control system, from this tank ammonia is pumped into the station's cooling loop which works on a similar principle as the cooling loop in the astronauts **LCVG** spider suit. Once the ammonia is warm it is rejected into space by radiators on the exterior of the ISS.

anomaly—something that is different from what is standard or expected, abnormal.

ascent procedures checklist—the checklist of tasks that each crew member on the flight deck must accomplish before the space shuttle's launch and during the ascent.

astronaut—a person trained to travel and work in space.

astrovan—a modified stainless-steel vintage Airstream RV that transports Astronauts from the Kennedy Space Center to the launch pad.

auxiliary power units—generated power to drive a **hydraulic pump** that produced pressure for the orbiter's hydraulic system—these systems helped position the nozzles of the space shuttle main engines so that the thrust of the engines can be directed for navigational purposes like the sails of a ship.

avionics—are the electrical systems used on spacecraft and aircraft. These include communication, navigation, monitoring, automatic flight control systems, etc . . .

Beanie Cap—the technical term for the cap was a gaseous oxygen vent arm. It covered the top of the external tank that supplied fuel to the space shuttle. The fuel in the tank was super-chilled liquid oxygen and hydrogen. The cap prevented the super chilled gas that evaporated from forming ice on the external tank that could break off and damage the shuttle.

centerline camera—is a piece of equipment installed in the shuttle **docking hatch** that helps the pilot and flight deck astronauts align the vehicle for docking.

chatter—electronic or radio communication.

closeout crew—are the people who strap the astronauts in and seal the access hatch before the space shuttle launch. The seven person crew includes two suit technicians from Johnson Space Center in Houston, three employees from Kennedy, one NASA quality inspector and an Astronaut Support Person, and an active astronaut who is not on the flight crew.

communications check—testing the space shuttle's ability to send and receive messages.

cosmonaut—an astronaut from Russia, they work together with Americans on the International Space Station.

countdown clock—at the Kennedy Space Center in Titusville, Florida, at the spectator grounds is a giant digital clock showing the hours, minutes, seconds and milliseconds until liftoff.

crew quarters—the home away from home for the crew of astronauts who are assigned to the mission.

cryogenic (super-chilled) liquid hydrogen fuel—is what propels the space shuttle's three main engines—it is the second coldest liquid on Earth at -423 degrees Fahrenheit (minus 252.8 degrees Celsius).

dock—physically attach with another vehicle in space.

drag—is resistance to motion in air. Like the friction generated when you try to scoot across a carpet (you could even get rug burn) there is a similar friction generated as a spacecraft or plane moves through the air, if the aircraft has a smooth surface like steel there will be less drag acting on it. If it is shaped in a way that will allow the air to be displaced easily around it, it will also experience less drag, think about how much faster a baseball or a paper airplane moves through the air after it's thrown than say, a plastic bag which traps air instead of displacing it.

drag parachute—helps the space shuttle come to a stop after landing by increasing drag.

egressing—is leaving an enclosed place (like a space shuttle).

emergency egress—a quick exit from a vehicle because of a dangerous situation requiring action right away.

emergency egress slidewire baskets—are the escape system of the launch pad, like lifeboats on a ship. These baskets are suspended on wires and slide down from the service structure (a steel tower 195 feet in the air that provides access to the shuttle) on the launch pad where the astronauts and closeout crew prepare for launch, to a safe distance away. These baskets slide quickly, up to 55 miles an hour!

engine bell nozzles—the nozzles of the space shuttle's three rocket engines were all shaped like bells. The engine burns the fuel and generates a lot of heat and pressure, the shape of the nozzle allows for maximum jet propulsion.

escape velocity—the speed needed for an object to break away from the gravitational pull of a planet or moon.

external tank—is the "gas tank" of the space shuttle, it contains the fuel and oxidizer used by the space shuttle main engines. Seventy miles above the earth the tank is detached from the shuttle and disintegrates as it falls through space, with the pieces eventually falling into the ocean.

extra-vehicular activities—include any activity done by an astronaut outside of a spacecraft beyond the earth's atmosphere. This is also called a spacewalk.

fallback area—a safe, three-mile distance from the launch pad, this is where the closeout crew and other NASA staff watch the countdown and launch of the space shuttle.

feed lines—carry the propellants (super-chilled) liquid hydrogen and oxygen from the external tank to the main engine.

flight engineer—is the member of the flight crew who monitors the computer and mechanical systems of the spacecraft that include, navigation, fuel, communications, etc.

flight-deck—referred to as a cockpit on an airplane, this is the uppermost section of the space shuttle where the pilot, commander and flight engineer sit as they fly the spacecraft.

force—is a push or pull.

fuel cells—generate electricity through a chemical reaction. In the orbiter Discovery's fuel cell oxygen and hydrogen react and convert chemical energy to electricity. Thermal conditioning is required to keep the oxygen and hydrogen cool in the cell.

fuel valve sensor—the engines of the space shuttle are combustion engines, like car engines, fuel is fed into the engine's combustion chamber (where it catches fire and powers the shuttle's flight) by a valve. This valve and its sensor are very important because the speed of the shuttle is determined by how quickly fuel flows into the engine (this why to speed up you step on the gas).

gauge—is an instrument for measuring something.

go-no-go decision—The controllers in the Launch Control Center monitoring the space shuttle's equipment and the flight conditions make a decision about the spacecraft's readiness and the weather conditions. This is called the Go-No-Go decision, either the necessary conditions for launch are met or they're not.

gravity—is the force by which a planet or other body draws objects toward its center.

hydraulic pump—a mechanical source of power that converts mechanical power into hydraulic energy (flow, or pressure). When a force is applied at one point by the pump it is transmitted at another point in the system by the fluid.

hydrogen igniters—It was normal for some of the liquid hydrogen fuel to evaporate (since the temperature at which it's liquid is −423 degrees Fahrenheit) but if there was too much, when the engine started the flammable gas could cause an explosion. The igniters were designed to burn off any gas that had evaporated before it was time to start the engines.

International Space Station (ISS)—is a satellite that orbits the earth, many of the world's nations collaborate on the station's construction and operation as a research laboratory, it is made up of fifteen modules, including living quar-

ters, labs, cargo bays and docks. Astronauts and cosmo-
nauts have lived and worked there since the year 2000.

Jet Propulsion Laboratory—located in Pasadena, California, which specializes in the development and operation
of unmanned rovers (robotically operated vehicles like
those that landed on Mars).

Johnson Space Center—is where astronaut space flight
training occurs. This means that any person selected as an
astronaut candidate needs to move to the Clear Lake City
area, a suburb of Houston, to begin the initial two-year
training program before they become eligible for a flight
assignment. It is also where Mission Control is located. You
may have heard the phrase, "Houston, we have a problem".

Kennedy Space Center—in Titusville, Florida, near Orlan-
do, specializes in prepping the space vehicles for launch
and is the location of NASA's launch pads.

knee boards—a miniature clipboard designed to fit on
your knee. **Astronauts** use them for their checklists.

ku-band antenna—provides high-rate communications
and television to the International Space Station.

laboratory—a room or building where scientific work is
done.

landing bag—contains the astronaut's passport, civilian
clothes to wear after landing, toiletries, etc. In case of an
emergency landing in another country, NASA staff will fly
the astronauts' landing bags to the astronauts so that
they can legally exit the country they land in and travel
back to the United States of America.

launch—to send something on its way, such as when a rocket's engines are ignited to send it from Earth into space

Launch Control Center—is where the spacecraft are checked out for the final time and given the "go" to launch. The NASA staff in the Launch Control Center monitor and supervise the launch.

Launch Entry Suit (LES)—this space suit protects the astronaut during the space shuttle launch and landing in case something goes wrong. The pieces of the suit, including the gloves and helmet, fit together so that none of the astronaut's skin is exposed. The suit is high tech, it provides oxygen for breathing, maintains air pressure, maintains body temperature and includes tools to help the astronaut escape if necessary (parachute, flotation device, radio, swiss army knife, flare gun, etc . . .)

launch pad complex—is the site of the rocket launch, it includes the launch pad where liftoff happens, the **Launch Control Center,** a news facility for the media and facilities to maintain the space shuttle.

launch pad—is the structure the shuttle assembly sits on, which is made of a special steel service structure that supported Discovery and allowed crew to access it in preparation for launch. The concrete pad itself is made of special material that is non-flammable. The space shuttle's engines and rocket boosters are combustion engines, they burn fuel and jets of fire propel the shuttle into space, the launch pad and service structure were built to withstand these flames.

launch window—this is the time during which the space shuttle must be launched, if complications prevent a launch, it will be postponed until the next launch window. The space shuttle's destination (the International Space Station) is not a spot on the map, it's a moving target orbiting the earth, so the launch window is calculated by NASA scientists at Kennedy with the International Space Station in mind as the moment when the space shuttle will be able to reach it in orbit.

life support system—is equipment that creates a comfortable environment by providing oxygen and by controlling temperature and air pressure.

Liquid Cooling and Ventilation Garment (LCVG)—is a spandex suit designed to be worn like long underwear, but instead of keeping warm it contains three hundred feet of tubing that circulates cool water to keep the astronaut from overheating. The suit also has a number of vents that draw sweat away from the body and that same sweat is then recycled in the liquid-cooling system.

main engine gimbal tests—the main engines were connected to the shuttle by a kind of bearing called a gimbal that allowed each engine to be pivoted to help steer the shuttle (the way sails are positioned to help to steer a sail boat).

Marshall Space Flight Center—in Huntsville, Alabama, is the heart of all engine development and testing.

maximum dynamic pressure or Max Q—the maximum pressure an object can withstand before it breaks.

microgravity—is the condition of being weightless, or of the near absence of gravity.

mid deck—the section of the cabin behind the flight deck, this is where the galley, toilet and sleeping area can be found, as well as the airlock.

mission—a special job given to a person or group of people.

Mission Control Center—After liftoff, mission control is handed off from the Kennedy Space Center in Florida where the launch takes place, to the Johnson Space Center in Houston. Mission Control is where every aspect of the shuttle's flight is monitored by NASA staff who also send commands to the space shuttle remotely to make sure the mission goes smoothly.

module—a self-contained unit of a spacecraft. The International Space Station is built of connected modules.

motion simulators—are machines astronauts use to practice before the mission, they create the feeling of being in exactly the same sort of motion they will experience during liftoff and space flight. The motion simulators allow the astronauts to build muscle memory that will allow them to perform all their necessary duties during the ascent and in space. NASA has the most sophisticated and largest motion simulators in the world, the **Vertical Motion Simulator** is in a tower ten stories tall.

Multi-Purpose Logistics Module (MPLM)—is a large, pressurized container used on space shuttle missions to transfer cargo to and from the International Space Station (ISS). From the module, supplies are offloaded, and finished experiments and waste are reloaded. The MPLM is then loaded back into the orbiter Discovery's payload bay for return to Earth.

muscle memory—is the ability to do an action without having to think of it, like catching a ball, playing piano or doing a cartwheel. Muscle memories are only formed with *a lot* of repetition. Practice allows the muscles to become used to specific movements, until these movements can be performed without conscious effort.

NASA—National Aeronautics and Space Administration.

nose cone—made of reinforced carbon—carbon, a material that can withstand temperatures of −3000 degrees Fahrenheit—this was the pointy front end of the orbiter Discovery. The nose of a plane is shaped like a cone to minimize the effect of drag on the space shuttle.

nozzle—a short, narrow tube that directs a flow or spray of liquid or gas. The space shuttle main engines have nozzles that shoot jets of gas from the combustion engine and power the shuttle's flight.

orbit—is the path followed by a moon, planet or artificial satellite as it travels around another body (like Earth) in space.

orbital velocity—the speed of a revolving object in a gravitational field (like the ISS or the orbiter Discovery). For the space shuttle to dock at the ISS it has to match the station's orbital velocity.

orbiter boom sensor—was a pole that attached to the end of the existing robotic arm on the International Space Station, a camera and laser on the boom's end allowed astronauts to check the orbiter Discovery's protective skin for possible damage that might have been sustained during the ascent.

orbiter docking system ring—was the docking mechanism on the space shuttle Discovery. It connected the orbiter to the ISS.

orbiter—was the part of the space shuttle that looks like an airplane. It flew into space and back down carrying people and equipment.

oxidizer—a type of chemical a fuel requires to burn, on Earth there is oxygen in the air which allows fire to burn but in space there is very little oxygen, so liquid oxygen was carried into space along with the shuttle's fuel, liquid hydrogen.

payload bay—the area inside the space shuttle orbiter where cargo was packed.

payloads—are cargo items carried into space by astronauts to help them complete their mission.

personal-preference kit—contains the non-essential personal items astronauts are allowed to bring aboard the space shuttle (it's a tiny bag).

portable heat exchanger—the LCVG pumps water through three hundred feet of tubing to keep the astronauts cool and this water gets quite warm in the process. While the astronaut is in the space shuttle for launch or landing, the suit is hooked into the life support system of the shuttle and the water is cooled by refrigeration. In the **Astrovan** and during spacewalks the water is cooled by a portable heat exchanger.

pressure leak test check—a test to make sure that the shuttle is air tight, even the tiniest hole can cause the shuttle to lose air pressure and make it difficult for astronauts to breathe.

pressurized mating adapter—was the mechanism that connected the port of the International Space Station to the docking port of the space shuttle.

propulsion—is the force that pushes forward or drives an object forward.

propulsion jets—generate thrust by ejecting a jet of air in the opposite direction of the vehicle.

pyrotechnic fasteners—the bolts that connected the **Solid Rocket Boosters** to the Space Shuttle were called pyrotechnic fasteners because they carried an explosive charge, the charge was ignited and the SRBs, the largest motors in human history, were separated from the space shuttle assembly.

quarantine—when a person's movement is restricted to prevent the spread of communicable diseases or infection.

Reaction Control System (RCS)—Jets were capable of providing small amounts of thrust in any desired direction or combination of directions. The RCS was also capable of providing torque to allow control of rotation (roll, pitch and yaw). The system used a combination of large and small (Vernier) thrusters, to allow different levels of response. Spacecraft reaction control systems were used for: altitude control during re-entry; maneuvering during docking procedures; "pointing the nose" of the space-craft; etc . . .

Remote Manipulator System—helped the orbiter get it's payload out of the bay with the use of an electromechanical arm and into the International Space Station.

remote sensing—is studying an object without coming into direct contact with it.

rendezvous—is an orbital maneuver during which two spacecraft, one of which is the International Space Station, arrive at the same orbit and approach until they are at a very close distance. Rendezvous requires a precise match of the orbital velocities of the two spacecraft, allowing them to remain next to each other. Rendezvous may or may not be followed by docking or berthing, procedures which bring the spacecraft in contact and link them together.

rocket—a vehicle used to launch people and objects into space.

roll, pitch and yaw—these are the words that describe the position of an aircraft in flight that allows it to be steered. Pitch is the movement of the plane up or down and can be seen by how its nose is pointed. Yaw describes the movement of the plane from side to side and can be seen by how its wings are positioned. A roll maneuver is when the plane turns over. Some maneuvers require a combination of adjustments to the plane's pitch, yaw and even roll. Such as the "thrust bucket" maneuver performed at Max Q.

saddle bag—contains the flight manual for Space Shuttle Discovery, the flight plan and other important materials for the flight engineer to have.

San Diego Chargers—a football team from San Diego that relocated to Los Angeles in 2017.

satellite—a natural moon or man-made object that orbits a planet or other object.

shuttle communication system—the system that allows the space shuttle to communicate with Launch Control and Mission Control, these systems are very sophisticated (there are no cellphone towers in space) and are developed at NASA's Glenn Research Center in Maryland.

shuttle's robotic arm—is a mechanical arm designed for grabbing, holding and moving objects.

Solid Rocket Boosters (SRBs)—are huge motors that give the space shuttle the extra power needed for liftoff, at 28 miles above the earth these motors detach from the space shuttle, descend with parachutes, are retrieved from the ocean by ship and then are refurbished by NASA for the next launch.

Soyuz—is a Russian spacecraft that carries people into space.

Soyuz seat liners—are made to fit using a mold of the astronaut's body, the Soyuz spacecraft are the only vehicle permanently docked to the International Space Station and all crew members of the ISS have a Soyuz seat liner in the event an escape becomes necessary.

space adaptation syndrome—(also known as space sickness) has similar symptoms to motion sickness, including nausea, vertigo and headaches. Just as while travelling in a car your body knows you're moving while you remain perfectly still in your seat, in space, your body needs to adjust to weightlessness.

space—is the area beyond the Earth's atmosphere, in space there is no air to breathe, but it is not true to say that space is empty, it contains dust, gases and bits of matter that float around as well as stars and planets.

space shuttle assembly—the orbiter Discovery, along with the machinery that needed to be attached to it so it could be launched into space, the solid rocket boosters and external tank that gave it the extra fuel and power needed to reach the stars.

space shuttle Discovery—was the size of a small jet, Discovery was a vehicle designed to carry astronauts and payloads into the Earth's orbit.

space shuttle main engines—there are three engines that power the space shuttle and along with the solid rocket boosters they provide the power for the space shuttle's liftoff and ascent into space.

Stepping Up Science—the name of our mission.

super-chilled liquid oxygen—must be combined with super-chilled liquid hydrogen fuel for it to burn; all fuel requires an oxidizer for combustion, on Earth the air contains enough oxygen for a log to catch fire in a fireplace but the Space Shuttle reaches a speed of 17,000 mph, and to do so it burns tens of thousands of gallons of fuel requiring an equally large quantity of oxygen.

thermal protection system—is a system used to protect spacecraft from temperatures that are too hot or too cold.

thrust—a forward or upward push.

Tracking and Data Relay Satellite system—is a network of American communications satellites and ground stations used by NASA for space communications.

vernier jets—a rocket engine on a space craft used by the pilot to make small adjustments to the attitude or velocity of the shuttle, it is especially useful in docking operations.

vertical launch position—is the position from which the space shuttle was launched.

White Room—where astronauts make final preparations before entering the spacecraft such as putting on helmets and parachute packs.

Photos